"The business knowledge collected and shared here by Davis and Cohen is simply invaluable; it's a must read for anyone who's in business to lead and succeed. If there were such a thing as an entrepreneurial gene, this book would be the map to its key components."

Ronald S. Lauder, Philanthropist, Ambassador, Chairman Of The Board Estee Lauder

"Having spent most of my career building entrepreneurial companies, I can say that Davis and Cohen hit the mark with The 24-Hour Turnaround. They use real life success stories to demonstrate that having a passion for the business, caring for people and focusing on the basics never go out of style."

George G Schwartz, Chief Operating Officer & Treasurer, Boston Private Bank & Trust Co.

"The 24-Hour Turnaround delves deeply into the nitty-gritty of entrepreneurial success. The case studies are fascinating and show how talent, inspiration, and some basic blocking and tackling can make a huge difference at an enterprise."

George Donnelly, Editor, Boston Business Journal

"At the end of the day, The 24-Hour Turnaround offers a rare brand of business-building advice: authentic ideas that have been road-tested by real entrepreneurs. Jeffrey Davis and Mark Cohen show how you can use the routes they've taken to create your own personal roadmap to success."

Josh Hyatt, Money magazine

"In The 24-Hour Turnaround, Jeffrey Davis and Mark Cohen have identified and unleashed principles of entrepreneurship that are applicable not just for small/mid-size companies, but also for large corporations. In fact, if more corporate executives empowered themselves to practice these principles, we could see major improvements in innovation, overall competitiveness, and social contribution from major companies."

Linne Kimball, Head of Licensing, Reebok International, Ltd

The 24-Hour Turnaround

How Amazing Entrepreneurs Succeed in Tough Times

**By Jeffrey S. Davis
and Mark Cohen**

20660 Stevens Creek Blvd., Suite 210
Cupertino, CA 95014

Published by Happy About®
20660 Stevens Creek Blvd., Suite 210, Cupertino, CA 95014
http://happyabout.com

First Printing: August 2011
Paperback ISBN: 978-1-60005-162-3 (1-60005-162-6)
eBook ISBN: 978-1-60005-163-0 (1-60005-163-4)
Place of Publication: Silicon Valley, California, USA
Paperback Library of Congress Number: 2011930596

Trademarks

Warning and Disclaimer

Jeffrey S. Davis would be pleased to hear from you.

Contact him at: JDavis@24-HourTurnaround.com.

The statements and opinions expressed in this book are those of the authors and do not necessarily reflect those of Happy About®.

Please note that it is the policy of Happy About to accept returns of any book the reader is not "happy about." If for whatever reason you are not happy with this book, please return it to us for a full refund.

Dedication

The inspiration for all good things comes from those closest to us.

With love,

Michael, Rachel, and Sandy

Stephanie, Joshua, and Wendy

Acknowledgments

Thanks to Jonathan Freedman, Bill Neumann, and Max Garfinkle for your help and support.

Special thanks to Harvey Chin and Tony Moureilles, our very talented cover and jacket designers.

Special love and thanks to Wendy and Sandy. Your help with the book was invaluable. We could not have done this without you.

Contents

Chapter 1   **Introduction to the 24-Hour Principles** **1**

Chapter 2   **When You Are Driven to Be the Best:**
Jerry Hyman, CEO, TriMark USA, Inc **7**

The Company Background: Small Family Business
to National Leader 8
The Development of the CEO 8
Problems and Challenges .10
Vision and Organizational Strategies 12
24-Hour Key Principle. 13
Leadership Style. 13
Communication Built on Trust 14
Message and Lessons 15
Summary 17

Chapter 3   **Turning Adversity into Competitive**
Advantage:
Karen Bressler, President and CEO,
AGAR Inc. **21**

The Company 21
The CEO. 22
AGAR's History. 23
Organizational Chaos. 27
Succession and Action Steps. 28
Leadership Style. 30
Lessons 31
Summary 33

Chapter 4   **From Humble Beginnings to a Market**
Leader:
Richard Cohen, CEO, Classico
Productions **37**

The Company. 37
The CEO. 37
Company's History 39
Getting Started 40
Problems and Challenges .40

Strategies and Action Steps. 41
Leadership Style 43
Message and Lessons. 44
Summary 47

Chapter 5 **Driven by Diligence, Loyalty, and Rewarding Excellence: Ken Ferry, CEO, iCAD, Inc.. . . . . 51**

The Company. 51
The CEO: Measurement Is Key and Everyone Counts 51
iCAD's History 52
Challenges and Problems 53
Importance of Being Visible 55
Strategies and Action Steps. 56
Organizational Philosophy 58
Communication and Meetings 59
Celebrating Accomplishments 60
Lessons 61
Acknowledgement for Success Well Earned 62
Summary 63

Chapter 6 **From Star Struck to Entrepreneurial Star: Joel Rabinowitz, CEO, The House 67**

The Companies 68
First Job: Record Store Manager/District Manager . 69
Second Business—"My own little agency". 69
Business Three: Things Really Take Off— Backstage Pass 70
The End of a Great Run. 72
Close a Door and Open Another 73
Business Four: The House—Friends Make Business Partners 73
The CEO 74
Like Father Like Son 75
Message and Lessons. 77
Summary 78

Chapter 7 **Using a Higher Purpose to Create Greatness: Russell Robinson, CEO, Jewish National Fund (JNF) 83**

The Jewish National Fund 83

The CEO. 83
Company History 85
Problems and Challenges 86
Strategic and Action Steps. 88
Taking Risks. 90
Leadership Style. 92
Message and Lessons 93
Summary 94

Chapter 8   **The Road to Success in 24 Hours 99**

Appendix A   **24-Hour Turnaround Scorecard 103**

Part I. 103
Part II 109

Authors   About the Authors. 115

Books   Other Happy About® Books. 119

Contents

Images

Image 1   Jerry Hyman the Leader 19

Image 2   Jerry with Restaurant Equipment 19

Image 3   Karen and Grandpa Karl 35

Image 4   Karen and Dad on Sideline at Patriots
Game Nov 2008 35

Image 5   Karen 36

Image 6   A Classico Event 48

Image 7   Another Classico Event 49

Image 8   Richard the Shining Star Behind
the Party 49

Image 9   iCAD Team at Times Square 65

Image 10   iCAD Team—Closing Bell at NASDAQ ..65

Image 11   Joel and Ringo 1989 80

Image 12   Paul and Joel 81

Image 13   Russell with Prime Minister Ehud
Olmert...96

Image 14   Russell with Prime Minister Yitzhak
Shamir 96

Image 15   Russell with Ronald Lauder 97

Image 16   Russell with Prime Minister Ariel
Sharon 97

1 Introduction to the 24-Hour Principles

The concept for this book started with the need for an answer to a critical question: Why in the most turbulent economy in eighty years, have some leaders of small and mid-sized companies demonstrated common traits that enabled them to perform exceptionally well and become leading companies in their fields?

Based on our years of experience and on-going research, we have chosen six outstanding entrepreneurs. Using their stories as told in their own words, we show how they progressed and led their companies to market leadership and un-imagined financial success. In this book, we identify the traits, which we call the "24-Hour Principles for Success." Our findings further showed that companies that focused on implementing these principles will start to see evidence of improvement within 24 hours.

We pay tribute to those people who are the unsung economic heroes of this economy. They are not the people you see or hear about in the news or the people you read about in magazines. Their organizations are not the part of the economy that got us into trouble. They are not making annual salaries that are more than we expect to make in a lifetime. These are the people who have built companies into regional, category, or national market leaders with lasting value.

You will not hear about these companies on CNBC or read about them in *The New York Times*. If you read the job reports you can see it is small and medium-sized businesses that are doing most of the new job creation. It is well documented that entrepreneurs are the engine that fuels job growth in this country. Government statistics show that about 75 percent of all new jobs come from entrepreneurial businesses. And while big companies shed jobs quickly, bowing to antsy shareholders, smaller firms are not afraid to start hiring when they find the best candidates. They lead the way out of the recession; they don't wait for a wave of improved economic news to carry them. Their ability to act and not just react fast is what this book is all about.

In talking about economic heroes we do not take the concept lightly or mean to minimize the courage of people who risk their lives to save others. Economic heroes are the people who have risked their livelihood, mortgaged their homes, sacrificed family and friends, and stepped into daunting situations and have as a result achieved levels of success most entrepreneurs dream of. They carry the weight of their employees and the businesses they serve. They create jobs, expand industries, and add to the quality of life of our society. As Benjamin Franklin said, "Energy and persistence conquer all things." In fact, Franklin is an example of an economic model citizen and entrepreneurial leader. He was practical, frugal, and ultimately through his multiple business ventures was a model entrepreneur.

These are stories of CEOs who have endured adversity and found ways to succeed. They felt the pain but kept finding ways to take stock of the world around them and kept re-inventing themselves. The stories come from our experience with over 700 companies spanning 25 years. The companies are public, private, family-operated, or non-profit. Companies like these are the basis of our economy. According to a recent Small Business Administration's Office of Advocacy survey, small businesses—firms with fewer than 500 employees—provide jobs for more than half of the nation's private workforce.

The leaders in the following chapters practice all of the 24-Hour Principles. Each chapter and person embodies these principles. They are all from different segments of the economy, industries, countries, and backgrounds. Each one practices these principles of leadership and management. Through intelligence, experience, integrity, and drive they have found the formula for success. They are the children and grandchildren of electricians, butchers, shop-owners, housekeepers, bookkeepers, managers, clerks, engineers, and even the children of Holocaust survivors. They are leaders who had the determination to overcome adversity and the self-confidence to inspire people to follow them. As you get to know where they came from and who they are today, we believe you will relate to them and learn what you need to do to succeed like them. In their own words, they will share about their roots, experiences, and the relationships that changed their thinking—and how this helped them achieve total success.

This book is about the kinds of companies most of us operate or work for and have no option other than to succeed. We hope you will implement the principals so that you can thrive as well. The chapters show how each company gained an advantage and learned how to win. As business advisors, we're often asked if people can change. The answer, of course, is that it depends, but the stories in this book show that anyone can adapt quickly and wisely, and ultimately win.

We want you to come away with an understanding of how to make quick and concrete change that you can start to implement in twenty four hours. These changes can have a lasting effect. We are presenting these stories of triumph and innovation as a practical prescription for entrepreneurial success in a turbulent economy.

We have provided a practical guide that is in an understandable format for entrepreneurial leaders to better diagnose themselves, their organizations, and their marketplace. This book will help you make the practical changes you will need to survive and thrive in the face of economic uncertainty.

Measuring your level of leadership and organization against the 24-Hour Turnaround Principles:

As you read the stories about the entrepreneurs in this book you will notice that each one has been scored against the principles of success of a 24-Hour Leader. All the entrepreneurs that we chose for this edition showed exceptional talent, determination, and values. Each one painted a unique entrepreneurial canvas and demonstrated their skills and success in their own unique fashion.

The final chapter of the book provides aspiring 24-Hour Leaders with a practical self-assessment tool to measure your own organization against the 24-Hour Turnaround Principles. These tools will give you an efficient way to get a snapshot of where your organization excels and where you should focus your time and attention to build a more outstanding leadership and growth organization. Our hope is that through understanding a specific aspect of each leader that we featured, you can then use the 24-Hour self-assessment tool and can begin to define a clearer path to your own remarkable results.

The 24-Hour Turnaround Principles include:

1. Vision and strategic plan that reflects the leader's personality, personal and family history, ambitions, goals, dreams, industry, and economic reality
2. Guiding principles and code-of-conduct that all employees know, understand, and follow
3. Relentless communication
4. Financial planning
5. Raising the bar—organizational and executive development as an essential element to success and leadership
6. Final decision maker, with the ability to gain support for tough decisions
7. Solicit help and support
8. Excellence from everyone—provide employees with tools and professional growth and development opportunities
9. Implement and use technology for monitoring, management, finance, and growth
10. Facilitate continuous positive action

Again, these principles are intended as the key elements of a practical prescription for entrepreneurial success in all business situations.

As you read each success story you will gain a more thorough understanding of the 24-Hour Principles and the elements for your success. At the end of each chapter we provide a score for that entrepreneur and highlight how their success reflects their application of the 24-Hour Turnaround Principles. The tools at the end of the book enable you to do exactly the same thing for your organization.

Chapter 1: Introduction to the 24-Hour Principles

2 When You Are Driven to Be the Best

Jerry Hyman, CEO, TriMark USA, Inc.
(http://www.TriMarkusa.com)

As soon as you meet Jerry you realize that he is a force to be reckoned with. He knows what he wants, he knows how to get it, and he will be relentless in achieving his objectives. His communications with his staff are in a type of shorthand in which he prefers concise messages that get right to the point. This philosophy is reflected in everything he does. It all seems remarkably simple and methodical.

Jerry is a leader who is calm, consistent, tough, and calculating. The nature of his business requires him to spend much of his time negotiating deals. He prides himself in being a hard and talented negotiator. He is also incredibly loyal. He gives, expects, and rewards loyalty, but that does not stop him from making difficult decisions. He has earned the respect of the people around him, both inside and outside TriMark, because they recognize that his goal is to get results and he stays laser-focused on achieving that goal. People who know Jerry say that you can see steely determination in his eyes. In a game of, "Who's going to blink first," it is a good bet that it won't be Jerry.

The Company Background: Small Family Business to National Leader

TriMark USA, Inc., formerly known as the United Restaurant Equipment Company, was founded in 1947 by Harry Halpern. Viewed as the best run company in its category, it is projected to soon become the country's largest provider of design services, equipment, and supplies to the foodservice industry. TriMark is committed to retaining its position as the market-leading supplier to independent restaurants. Jerry started as a sales person in the showroom, and over two decades he worked his way up through the company's ranks to become president of TriMark United East in 2000. In 2005 he became president and CEO of TriMark USA. TriMark provides foodservice operators with solutions to their most complex requirements. Today the company earns approximately $600 million in revenue in 13 offices nationwide. Since the economic crisis that began in 2008, the company has grown while the rest of the industry has contracted. The company has added over 150,000 square feet of warehouse space in three different locations.

TriMark employs kitchen engineers and interior designers who draw the plans and specify the products to accomplish their mission of supplying everything that goes into a restaurant. You can eat at a restaurant every night of the week and never know the name TriMark. It's not a marquee business. They live in the background but they supply everything that you see in a restaurant from the physical plant and equipment to all the china, glassware, linen, etc.

The Development of the CEO

"I knew from an early age that I wanted to be a businessman. I always was going to be the guy who worked in an office and had a briefcase. I had a lot of awards and recognition as I was growing up. I won the Congressman's Medal of Honor. My parents were, of course, very proud. Because of all my accomplishments, I got a lot of positive feedback." Jerry was a psychology major at Cornell. During college he worked, but was trying to figure out what he wanted to do with his life.

"I was the first in my family to go to an Ivy League school. My last two years at Cornell I was a bartender to make extra money. My parents paid for my education and weren't wealthy. After I graduated, I sent out my resume and tried to find a job in psychology, without much success. The guy that I was working for as a bartender offered to take me in as his partner. The deal was that I would open additional bars with him, with no investment, just sweat-equity. He had access to capital, and he said, 'I will take you in as a full partner. I have enjoyed working with you these last two years. Let's go out and open some more college bars.' I was 21 and this all sounded pretty cool to me. So I did it. I said, 'Mom, Dad, I'm not coming home from Ithaca, I'm going to stay here, and I'm going to run bars.' Of course their reaction was, 'We just spent $45,000 dollars to send you to Cornell and you're going to be a bartender?' I said, 'Yup, that's what I'm going to do.' As you can imagine, that didn't go over very well."

Similar to other leaders in this book, Jerry demonstrated the 24-Hour leadership characteristics early in his career. Jerry stood out as a 22-year-old partner in several bars, he was a young kid with a lot of money.

"I bought myself a Fiat Spider convertible. I had an apartment in Ithaca and another in Binghamton and even found time to work on my MBA. It was an amazing lifestyle. The bar at Ithaca would close at 1 a.m. I would cash out and work with the employees to clean up. Then I'd get in my car at 1:30 a.m. and drive to Binghamton, and I'd be in Binghamton at 2:30, just in time for that bar to close at 3. I would cash out, and close the bar around 3:30 in the morning... At the time, I carried a gun in the glove box of the car because I would make the bank deposit and had to be in a position to protect myself. What you read is true. People wait for the guy coming out of the bar at 3 o'clock in the morning with the bag of money."

Jerry became immersed in a fantasy lifestyle of fast everything. But in the end, all of it was burning him out. The fast cars, fast life style and endless days and nights were starting to lose the sizzle and it was not working for him anymore, he knew that it was time for a drastic change.

"After four years, I sold my share to my partner. I packed up my stuff and went home. I tried to think of what I wanted to do. I found myself thinking about what I liked over the last three or four years in running these bars. It occurred to me that what I liked best was the process of planning, designing, and building the new establishments. That's what I found really exciting."

"One day I noticed an ad in the newspaper for a restaurant supply company in North Smithfield, RI, a family-owned business called United Restaurant Equipment Company. It was an ad for an entry-level position to work at the counter in the showroom. I interviewed with Bob Halpern, the founder's son. Bob said, 'Okay, let me get this straight. You're applying here for an entry-level position, which pays minimum wage, to work at the counter in the showroom. You have an Ivy League degree. You have two-thirds of your MBA done. You've run successful businesses as an owner. And you're going to come to work in an entry-level position?'"

This was the job that Jerry was looking for and he made his case. He made it clear that for him, this job was not about money or title. Most importantly, with supreme confidence he made the point that, if given the chance, he would be a great asset to the company and would move up the corporate ladder. Jerry was hired and over time his plan became reality.

"I started working in the showroom in 1981, and I've been with the company ever since. At the time the company was doing about $10 million and now it is over $600 million. I have worked in every department. It was a small company, maybe 40 employees and I did everything. I got the trucks out in the morning. I worked in the estimating department and then became the sales manager. Eventually I was the head of customer service, vice president of sales, general manager, and then president. I just worked my way up."

Problems and Challenges

"We try to get people to realize they should let the family move on in life. Sometimes, though, families hold on. And then they have nothing."
- Joel Getzler, Family business consultant

Even under the best of circumstances, family-owned businesses are a challenge. It's impossible to separate the family dynamics from the business. The business will always reflect the family for better or for worse.

Jerry worked hard to develop superior work habits and as a result he stood out. He arrived daily at work at 7:40 a.m. reviewing overnight shipping reports and meeting with his senior VPs before returning to study sales, back-orders, and cash and receivables reports.

"After a number of years, I was the only executive that was a non-family member. So I dealt with all those organizational issues." As the company grew, the family made the decision to sell TriMark to a private equity company. "Bob Halpern became CEO of the parent company, and went out and began to try to acquire other companies. When Bob became CEO, I became president of TriMark. That was very difficult." Part of the difficulty was that Jerry was promoted over family members already in the business, so there was lots of tension.

Under Jerry's astute leadership the business continued to grow and change. More acquisitions were on the horizon and members of the family were being passed over as Jerry gained more authority. Jerry was gaining more power and control. On the surface this was not a situation in which there appeared to be issues between family members and non-family executives.

"We acquired four companies, and then in 2000, 2001 the economy changed. The company had grown from about $10 million when I started to close to $60 million. Then after acquiring the four companies, we grew to about $125 million, both through organic growth and acquisition. Then the acquisitions stopped. But we continued significant organic growth. After about five years or so our equity owners decided that it might be a good time to sell us. We were at about $175 million in sales."

"Bob was in his mid-60s. He built a home in Florida, was semi-retired and eventually retired completely. I became CEO of TriMark USA on March 1, 2005, and around that time we were sold to the Audax Group, so we had a new infusion of capital."

Jerry was a keen student and gained a lot of valuable experience and perspective on the industry and the sale of the company that he would use again and again to his advantage. "Prior to the sale, I gave many management presentations to the suitors. The audiences ranged from big box home improvement chains who thought they might like to get into the restaurant supply industry to our competitors. I presented to a huge number of Wall Street folks and all kinds of private equity companies. What I found is that food service operations is an industry that everybody can relate to. Everybody has a favorite restaurant. When I explained to people what we do, they realized that they simply hadn't thought about how a restaurant comes into being. They hadn't thought about the fact there is a company and an entire industry that has kitchen engineers and interior designers who draw the plans and specify the products. Companies like mine supply everything that goes into the restaurant and then handle all of the re-supply needs, the china, the glassware, the pots, and the pans. When you're in a restaurant, everything that you see comes from a restaurant equipment and supply company. People get into that, especially these days with all of the celebrity chefs. They get it and they say, 'Wow, that's pretty neat...here's a company that creates all these restaurants.'"

Vision and Organizational Strategies

From the beginning Jerry's vision has been for TriMark USA to be the largest equipment and supply dealer in the world. In 2009 they were number two and clearly moving in on the number one position. The company strategy included consistent, concise, and clear communication that supported improved productivity at all levels. A guiding principle was to ensure that the company's employees were all aiming for the same target. Achieving this goal and doing it as a company-wide initiative is clearly a point of emphasis for Jerry.

24-Hour Key Principle

Leadership Style

Being CEO was a different kind of transition than Jerry was prepared for. "Nobody taught me how to be a CEO. I didn't go to CEO school. It's interesting how different kinds of people progress in their careers. Some people intuitively know what to do. Other people may not have that same intuition, but they're smart, they read a lot of books, and they watch successful people. I have 13 division presidents that work for me. A long time ago I made a decision that I would suggest that one of these presidents take over my position. You have to understand that these are all very strong leaders. Some of them are running $100 million-dollar divisions. The one that I chose is the one that gets it intuitively. They all do a very good job, but some have to work harder at it. Having said that, these things are not absolutes. Almost everybody can improve and perhaps through reading you can actually elevate your abilities. I am currently reading *My American Journey* by Colin Powell."

"I hire smart people. As you walk around here [TriMark Headquarters], one of the things that you will see is that I like calm. I am a calm person. I never yell. I don't lose my temper. I like things neat. And I like to be in control. With this division, I still sign every check by hand, as do all of my division presidents. Every check that goes out, for this $600 million-company, is signed by hand."

"I do not write memos or send long emails. I keep things concise. I don't issue policies. I don't have a written strategy sitting in the drawer. I talk to people. There are lots of other things I do to keep things simple. I do not have a secretary. I schedule my own appointments and make my own travel arrangements."

Jerry's drive to lead by example and unique, personal style is always evident. He keeps things simple and consistency is apparent in everything he does. "I am fortunate, especially with all the division presidents we have today, since I am not only the CEO of TriMark USA, but I also still hold the position of president of the largest operating division. The division presidents relate not just to what I say, but also to what I do."

"When I visit one of the TriMarks, like the four that I went into last week, I never walk in the front door. I always walk in through the warehouse. I don't announce myself to the receptionist. They're TriMarks, and I am the CEO, so I come in like any other employee comes in. I will wander around the organization, and people know me because I visit them a lot and I talk to them. After I have been through the whole company, then I will show up in the president's office. By doing that, I get to see what goes on in the organization. I get to speak to people before I speak to the division president."

Communication Built on Trust

Jerry embodies the 24-Hour Principles in that he practices good communication and people development with a passion. "They are not afraid to tell me anything because I just talk to them. When I was out in the warehouse, the warehouse guy said that we have done a poor job with the new racking. So I walked around and looked at it and I realized that we could do better. Getting people to be open with you is not so hard. Remember, I have worked for this company for 28 years. People tell me things."

The total commitment to loyalty that Jerry shares with all his employees does not come without a big personal sacrifice. He takes very seriously the unwritten agreement he has with his team. He holds the bar higher than others, communicates his expectations clearly, provides for development and measures what is done. As a result he expects them to do their very best and in return he provides a special environment for work in an industry where that has not been the standard.

Jerry has a commitment to developing people. "One thing I am really big on is trying to develop people from within the company. We have a great many people who are now sitting at desks who worked in the warehouse. We have people who were receptionists who are now buyers. I believe in cross-training people and trying to move them along within the company. The head of our customer service department is a woman who's worked here for 18 years. She came to see me the other day. By the way, everybody knows they can always come and see me because I have no secretary. There's no one to make an appointment with, so you just come and see me. She asked me if she could discuss the possibility of becoming an outside territory salesperson. It was a huge difference for her. She thought that she might like to become a straight commission road salesperson. This means she would be calling on restaurants in a territory. She wanted to discuss it with me. After an hour and a half, we decided that it's something that she should do after 18 years with the company. Good for her, but good for me, too, because that's where the company gets its money from. And if she's successful in doing that, then she can double her pay, because it's straight commission, and if she does, I'll be the happiest guy in the world to give her the check."

There are lots of joys associated with success, but with this kind of growth inevitably comes the challenge of jobs that expand beyond the scope of the incumbent. The challenge for a leader is always to handle these situations humanely, but quickly.

"We had a division controller who was one of the hardest working guys in the company, but he was unable to grow as the company grew. The way that he tried to mitigate that was by working longer and longer hours. The guy would be here non-stop. He'd start at four in the morning and he'd be here until seven at night, and it was just getting worse and worse. Finally I had to let him go for his own good and for the good of the company."

Message and Lessons

"When we're looking to acquire companies we visit a lot of different sites. As you can imagine, to acquire eight companies, I probably looked at 80. I have a bit of a ritual that I follow when I'm talking to the president of a company I'm interested in. When I go to their office, I might say to the person, do you save any of your voicemails? Sometimes people save an old voicemail for a reason. Sometimes it's a good reason, sometimes it's a bad reason. But I found that it's an interesting dynamic. They've saved those voicemails for some reason and it tells me a bit about them. I'll say to the person, would you mind if I hear the kinds of voice mails you've chosen to save?"

Jerry's own saved voicemails were instructive as well. There was a warehouse worker thanking Jerry for a recognition award he received, a thank-you from a salesperson they just hired, a chef who would like to do business with TriMark. Of the twelve others about half were messages of appreciation in one form or another. Jerry also saved many thank you notes from people he had helped.

"There's a lot of respect there and appreciation. That applies to my competitors as well. The last voicemail is from my chief competitor. He's calling to ask me a question."

Jerry sees life as a continuous learning process and does not feel he has to follow a prescribed method to learn things. "I did not take a textbook route to the top. I never finished my MBA. I was almost done, but I didn't finish. I've always been big on learning. I attend a lot of seminars and I have a lot of board positions. But on a day-to-day basis, I use my undergraduate degree in psychology far more than I use what I have learned in business school. The ability to read people, understand someone's motivation, understand my own psychology and what motivates me is amazingly helpful in running a large company."

For someone who is as driven and focused on personal contact as Jerry, the inherent solitude of the CEO role could be a problem. His commitment to spend so much time at each of TriMark's thirteen facilities means lots of time on planes and in hotel rooms and yet with Jerry there's always a thought-out plan.

"I am not lonely. The division presidents and I are all contemporaries. We are all friends, even though I am the boss. We grew up in the industry together. We do things socially together. This year will be our third annual sailing trip. I'm leaving in August to sail to Windsor, Ontario, which is a big sail. We are going to sail from Cleveland to Ontario and back."

Still directly involved with the business, Jerry will personally supervise a restaurant project.

"I worked with Todd English, who has since become quite a national celebrity chef, and his wife when they opened the first Olive's. It was a tiny little restaurant. I chose to work personally on these projects for a number of reasons. First, if I get personally involved, it's a good barometer for me to know how the company is performing. Even though everyone in this company will know this is a 'Jerry' project, you can only hide so many sins. It also lets me know how our estimating department, our project managers, our receiving department, our equipment installers, and billing departments are doing. So I get to see how the whole company is functioning. Second, if I personally am going to be involved in helping somebody open a restaurant, I better know what I am talking about. I had better not let the industry slip by me. I could stay in my office all day long reading this junk. And third, is that it is really fun. It is fun to be involved with the opening of the next hot restaurant in town."

Another 24-Hour Principle that Jerry lives by is that high expectations start at the top. He is a model for leadership as he consistently demonstrates an unstoppable desire to be directly involved in everything, to know every detail. This is part of Jerry's self-confessed desire to be in control, but it is also about modeling to everyone high standards and personal integrity. He was recently elected president of the largest and oldest buying group called Allied Buying Corporation (ABC). It's an organization composed of the 60 best companies in the industry. It's an elected position, elected by the other people in the group. It points to his uncanny ability to be both a fierce competitor and a respected colleague. "Why would they want me as president? As much as they may recognize me as a tough competitor, I assume they also respect me as a leader and strong representative of the group."

"It's very easy to explain. I may be everybody's friend. Maybe some people look up to me. They may think I'm honest and I do what I say I am going to do. But TriMark's the enemy. All our competitors are trying to grow their companies, they are trying to hold onto their customers and get new customers. But there is a balance. This is a buying-group-driven industry. These groups are the vehicle where we get most of our profit dollars because they offer vendor rebates and discounts."

Summary

Jerry Hyman is a complicated leader. He's fierce, compassionate, and highly principled. He's ferociously driven, but he never raises his voice. He thrives in controlled chaos, and is supremely calm. He likes being in charge of a big enterprise, but he books his own travel, answers his own phone, and schedules his own appointments. He likes having power, but he adores the fact that a warehouse worker will call to thank him for a recognition award. Part of Jerry's formula for success is that he knows just about everything that's going on at TriMark almost all the time. He holds himself and others to the highest of standards, but has the ability to communicate and relate to people at all levels. He also is a keen student of his industry and knows what his competitors are up to today and can predict with a high level of certainty what they are planning for tomorrow. He knows these things because he is an exceptionally good listener and obsessively pays attention to everything that goes on around him. Jerry makes all he does seem relaxed and simple, and the key to his success is his combination of experiences and skills and an unrelenting desire to do better every day.

Author's 24-Hour Turnaround Score: 92

Jerry's 24-Hour Leadership Principles:

∞ The leader that you are today is the sum of everything that's happened to you up to this point

∞ Communication is a core philosophy—it drives organization structure, staff, and strategy

∞ Remain calm, never yell, don't lose your temper

∞ Develop people from within—use cross-training to move people within the company

∞ Do not hesitate to make unpopular decisions

∞ Be accessible to everyone—be sure employees aren't afraid to tell you anything

∞ Keep all communication crisp and brief

∞ Always have a long-range strategy—it doesn't have to be written

∞ Do everything possible to meet new employees and know them by name

∞ High performing people and teams know that it's important to never stop learning

Image 1: Jerry Hyman the Leader

Image 2: Jerry with Restaurant Equipment

Chapter 2: When You Are Driven to Be the Best

3 Turning Adversity into Competitive Advantage

Karen Bressler, President and CEO, AGAR Inc. (http://www.AGARsupply.com)

The Company

AGAR is a privately held company, headquartered in Taunton, MA. The company is a broadline distributor of primarily wholesale beef, pork, lamb, veal, sausage, poultry, seafood, and produce.

Today AGAR is the largest independent wholesale food distributor in New England. It has served New England grocery stores, restaurants, chain stores, and other retail food industry customers for over 70 years. Its current president and CEO, Karen Bressler, has gained local and national recognition as a business leader, female entrepreneur, and executive. Until she re-married, she was a dedicated single mother. In 2007 Karen won The Ernst & Young Regional Entrepreneur of the Year award. She speaks six languages, one of the many qualities that make her stand out as a truly unique 24-Hour leader.

The CEO

Karen's Progression at AGAR:

∞ Joined Genoa Sausage, a division of AGAR, doing general administration and sales work

∞ Management trainee

∞ Corporate Credit Manager

∞ Foodservice Sales Representative

∞ Sales Manager, Retail Asian Department

∞ Executive Vice President

∞ President

∞ CEO

∞ Current: President and CEO

Karen is tireless in mission and purpose. She survived adversity and brought innovation, vision, and social responsibility to the family's business. After years of working successfully in many positions at AGAR, today Karen is the president and CEO of the family-owned business that has grown from a small niche meat supplier to a broadline distributor that has strategically added key personnel as well as new specialty product areas. AGAR has emerged to become the acknowledged regional leader and nationally recognized organization in its market. The transition was both personal and professional and took Karen from the depths of corporate and personal despair to being the clear market leader and a person her peers hold as a model of entrepreneurial leadership. Her story is one of transformation and triumph over predatory competitors, loss of key talent, the need to shed unprofitable business lines and an equally pressing need to add new, more profitable ones. At the same time, she never stopped maintaining a strong, loving and professional relationship with her father and family. As an executive who was also a single mother, she was consistently focused on the well-being of her daughter no matter what else was going on. It's easy to see why Karen was chosen as a 24-Hour Leader.

AGAR's History

The background of the company is a mix of a movie script and shrewd entrepreneurship. AGAR was incorporated in 1940, but its legacy goes back well before that. Karen's grandfather was a kosher butcher. After an argument with the local rabbi, her grandfather no longer sold kosher meat and started selling pork to the merchants he knew well in Boston's Chinatown. He also started a meat cutting operation in Boston, called Trimright, at 2 ½ Blackstone St. in Boston. The "½" meant that they occupied a basement location.

The business evolved and had its ups and downs with Karen's grandfather. It was eventually passed on to Karen's father Alan. Alan—a natural entrepreneur—looked for new ways to grow and develop the business platform he took over. "My father was a talented entrepreneur and he used AGAR as the springboard to develop different kinds of ventures. Some were very successful, some not so successful."

"Originally my father didn't want to bring any of his children into the business." Karen never aspired to working at AGAR either. "I was the only one of my siblings who went to business graduate school, and I studied international business. That's what I really wanted to do." But as time progressed her father realized that it would be good for the business to bring one of his children into AGAR to manage and protect the business legacy.

Karen had a progression of positions at AGAR. Around 1992, she was doing administrative and sales work at a division of AGAR called Genoa Sausage. Her next position was as AGAR's first management trainee. Since there was no formal training program, she was moved around the company and worked in various departments including the warehouse, sales, purchasing, and then going on the road with truck drivers and brokers. One Monday the whole foodservice sales department failed to show up for work. They had all taken jobs with the competition. Karen was immediately taken out of her training program and became a foodservice sales rep. She was learning by doing, but was restless and felt she was ready for a position of greater responsibility. Around that time, Karen's father was visited at AGAR by food industry icon Frank Perdue. Frank talked to Alan about how Frank's son had a growing involvement in Perdue Farms. Alan had Karen come to his office where he introduced her to Frank. After Perdue left Karen went to see her father and said, "I need more responsibility. I am not just a doll that you can dust off the shelf so you can show me to people." Her point was made.

"In the late 90s we did some strategic planning. My father was thinking about what he wanted to do next. We studied the market and realized there was an opportunity for an independent broadline seller in New England." At that point Karen held the title of Executive Vice President. "We didn't have the right facility in Boston to do that kind of business. We studied the situation and my father decided that it would be best to move our facility to Taunton, MA. Unfortunately it was such a complicated move that it almost killed the business and all of us with it. Her succession to CEO was just six months after overseeing the move to a new facility 35 miles south from their original location."

"The new site was three times larger than the original building. This move enabled AGAR's expansion into new categories, such as frozen foods, condiments, sauces, flour, cheeses, paper, and cleaning supplies. These are all the product lines needed for broadline distribution to the foodservice industry (restaurants, sub shops, home meal replacement, assisted living facilities, etc.)."

"The beginning was a disaster and many things associated with the move went wrong:

1. Prior to the move we bought a produce business from a competitor who had gone under.
2. We purchased a pizza/sub distributor.
3. We were in the process of converting our ERP system software.
4. Our financial tracking system was outdated.
5. The current management team was in over their heads."

"These all put different demands on the business and all required cultural changes that required skills and experience we didn't necessarily have."

"As a result of moving 35 miles south of Boston, they lost many employees. Some left because of the new location, but most left because of instability about where the new, expanded business was headed. On paper the move to Taunton was a good long term strategy, but the timing was off and in retrospect it made things a lot harder. "The building was not complete on moving day so products could not be brought in fast enough. Construction workers had to finish their job, but they were in the way (AGAR is a 24/7 business). Trucks were loaded improperly because of changes in operations and as a result, drivers were not able to service customers correctly, which added to everyone's frustration. Morale was at an all time low and right at that time, Teamsters Local 25 petitioned AGAR. Vendors were spreading false rumors that we were not paying bills and were on shaky ground. The rumors about bills were false, but it was true that we were under pressure from the bank."

Her father was a very successful entrepreneur whose passion was finding and developing new and thriving businesses. Like a true entrepreneur, he was pulled in many directions and was focused on many projects in different stages of development. AGAR was struggling and the day-to-day operations required obsessive attention to detail. The business was bleeding money and there were long-tenured employees who were no longer getting the job done. Karen felt it would be better for her to step up and take the initiative to address these personnel issues rather than to ask her father to do that. Since Karen saw her future as the leader, she felt the current instability made it a good time for her to accelerate her leadership progression and make her move and lead the company out of its problems. Alan believed in Karen and in 2001 Karen became the CEO of AGAR. She knew she was not fully ready, but in the best interests of the business and her family, she accepted her new leadership role. From the moment Karen took charge, the struggles continued and actually got worse with customer service issues, organizational leadership changes, transitioning from old to new product lines, attrition, and low morale. As a result, the financials continued to suffer and AGAR was in survival mode.

"My goal was to live through the day. I wanted to just not go out of business. That was my strategy. I kept saying, 'I can't fail. Failure is not an option.' There was a group of very loyal people at different levels of the company who stepped up and who were very helpful in terms of carrying out our objective. They were turning the wheels in the background to keep things going. There were also new people that we had brought in who were working very, very hard. Some had left another company to come here. Fortunately a lot of people stepped up to make this work."

"History worked in our favor. The fact that we were a meat company allowed us to build on our core strength. Meat is the most expensive portion of a meal. We also have all the ancillary items around that and that gave us a way to maintain cash flow."

Despite professional and personal pressures, Karen had a strategic vision for AGAR. Under her leadership AGAR was re-inventing itself. To build awareness of the changes, Karen dedicated herself to spending more time meeting with customers. As CEO, she wanted her employees and customers to feel like they were dealing with a different kind of food distributer. It took a while for everything she wanted to do to all fall into place, but as she looks back today, she can describe what she meant by the phrase, "being a different kind of supplier."

"We try to make everything we do look different and better. Having me as President/CEO means the leadership looks different. We try to show that we are different for a reason. Our offices look special, they're more fun. Our customers are surprised to see things like this big neon cow we brought into the trading pit."

Karen worked hard at improving the work environment. Ironically, though she introduced the theme of fun at work, she was under tremendous stress. There were many changes going on simultaneously. On the family side, it meant allowing her father to comfortably transition out of the running of the business. It also meant attending to the needs and being the primary support for her daughter. On the business side, it meant raising the bar for a conventional food company and in doing so, building a management team that could operate at a very high level. "Change is difficult in a traditional business like ours. Our business works on the smallest of profit and there was little margin for error. I was also dealing with changes in key personnel at all levels and as a result had to make many complex and often unpopular decisions."

Organizational Chaos

The new facility created a whole new set of problems. They had not yet properly staffed the new roles that expansion had created. The fact that people were quitting on a daily basis only added to the confusion. In an industry that looked like a good old boy's network, Karen stood out like a sore thumb.

"I felt like an employee before. I had to have humility coming in the door as the owner's daughter. I just put my head down and plowed ahead. I had to prove myself. I worked hard and showed that I had it. It was important to me to make a contribution. What changed as CEO was that I suddenly realized that everybody was expecting me to pull them out of the mess we were in. I had to make decisions and essentially say, 'Do it this way.' I had to stand up and just make the damn decision because nobody else wanted to do it. This was a very lonely and difficult time. I was in an abyss, and there was just no way out. There was an immense amount of pressure and stress. The chaos was still all around us for a long period of time. It was years of craziness. Many times it felt like we should just give it up."

Despite the turmoil, Karen was focused on implementing her vision for the company. "I was determined to be an innovator in an industry allergic to innovation. I wanted a direct, open, face-to-face style of management where people worked their issues openly and collaboratively. I wanted to be able to give and get honest feedback."

Karen knew that the only way things would change was to state clear and consistent leadership goals for her and her team. More importantly, become a role model for those goals with her staff. "I accepted the fact that I was not going to be loved by all the people around me, but I also knew that if my team experienced some success under my leadership, that things would start to turn around and the majority of people would start to follow. Then we would be in a position to build for the future."

Succession and Action Steps

Karen felt the burden of being the CEO. Each day she carefully calculated the decisions she had to make and was gaining the respect of the management team. Her father had handed the day-to-day operations of the business over, but after all his years in the business, his actions showed that at times he was finding it hard to let go. Karen admired her father and respected his judgment and liked having him as an advisor, but she needed to establish some ground rules between them. She finally said, "You know what Dad, you can't call me all the time on my way to work anymore, because it takes all of my energy to walk in that door and do what I do under these circumstances. When I talk to you I feel down and it's very hard to get myself back up. I will update you, and I won't hide anything."

"Setting rules with her father was a difficult and important step. One-by-one I was prioritizing the problems and taking action to make things better and more systematic. I made unpopular decisions, but I explained to people why I made them and even if they didn't like it, they at least understood my thinking. If it's really unpopular, I've encouraged my team to come tell me why they think I'm wrong and propose a better solution."

"I was recently speaking at a conference in Chicago and described my management style. I surprised some when I told them about how I invite criticism and feedback. When they questioned how I deal with this criticism, I said, 'If they don't tell me what they think, I won't trust them to be honest with me.' The value is that we 'duke it out, and even if, in the end, I decide we're still doing it my way, I really enjoy the benefit of being challenged. Often I find that somebody might have thought of something I didn't think of. I don't want them to stay quiet. There's a lot of things I thought of doing that were really unpopular and either the team convinced me that it was not a good idea or they got behind me and understood after we debated it, that it was."

Another value that Karen encouraged her staff to practice was the concept of empathy. It didn't matter to her what position a person had in the company. The rules were applied equally:

1. Listen carefully to understand the other person's perspective
2. Be sure you understand their point-of-view
3. Explain what the final decision is and why

By using this communication style, Karen was able to help her managers get comfortable with the idea that AGAR was going to be a different kind of food distributor. They were going to do what was right for the company and for each other and in doing so they would be developing a more productive culture.

Karen's management style was starting to become the accepted norm. At this point the balancing act was to keep the business headed in the right direction, stay actively involved as a mother, and keep her father informed on the businesses progress. As AGAR was still not out of the woods, she was concerned that her father would not be comfortable with her as CEO. "I was not beloved. That was stressing my Dad."

Customer care during the worst times was key. "Our competition knew we were in trouble, they smelled blood. They all came after us. That's a daily event, still today. They were all spreading rumors that we were going out of business. As a result, I spent a lot of time meeting with people to tell them that we were going to be fine. The broker community is very prolific in their gossip, and a broker told a major customer that we were going down. So I had to set some rules and tell the broker that I would not tolerate that." One of Karen's 24-Hour leadership skills was that she understood the power of personal relationships. When she was able to spend time with customers the relationships worked. The challenge was prioritizing the chaos.

Dealing with attrition was a concern. "Brokers were also calling employees, telling them that AGAR was going out of business. I had managers quitting on a daily basis. The head of one division quit. So I ran that division. Then somebody else would quit, and my reaction was okay I'll do that job too. As a result, every morning there was a line of people outside my door. I'm glad those days are over, things are much better now."

Getting the right people into the right positions was a priority. "Once we had the right staff in place, we could put our heads down each day and focus on one big problem at a time. With success, morale rose. Also, many of those with a poor attitude left the company. Having new employees, with fresh attitudes, made for a better environment. As AGAR's profits and growth started to come back, the team was excited to continue on this path. We implemented lots of new strategies to get more customers and provide more items."

"A sign of the company's growing health was when capable people left the company and it wasn't quite as traumatic as it used to be. In fact, it got to the point that I could help people to leave, if that was the best option for everyone." Over time her confidence grew and she learned to trust her instincts, speak her mind, and accept help from trusted advisors. "There are people I trust who I consult with if I've made an unpopular decision. I would call and say I did this and everybody hates me for it and we would work through the crisis together. It helps having someone you trust to go to."

Leadership Style

Part of Karen's transition as a 24-Hour top leader was building confidence that her personality and perspective were going to set the right tone for the company. "If I came in and looked worried, then everyone else would sense that panic. If I communicated that I thought the business was going to be there forever, then it made it easier for people to focus on the problems of the day."

Hiring people who fit with Karen's team meant these new hires had to be in sync with her commitment to superior communications. "I disseminate a lot of information and ideas that I read. I email it around, and that's become contagious and a lot of us now do it. It helps everyone. I'm a reader and I encourage others to do that as well. The philosophy of, 'I want to be the smartest one here' doesn't really jibe with me."

In addition to common values, Karen wanted to hire good business people who had a strong sense of group accomplishment and accountability. "Incentives are based on results. Part of our philosophy is that we need to achieve our goals together. If you, as a senior manager, didn't hit your numbers but the company did and we think that you have contributed to the whole picture, then you'll still get a bonus. We try to be holistic about it. It might be a reduced incentive, but it's not an all or nothing."

"Money is our survival on a day-to-day basis. AGAR is here, but it's not because we're cute and sell pretty dresses. It's because we understand this business and can manage very thin margins. You perish tomorrow if you can't provide the top service and product while we whittle that tiny little margin out. It is a fine balancing act."

"We made a strategic decision. When gas prices doubled, we made the choice to have AGAR not follow the competition but rather show our customers our dedication to them and absorbed a significant portion of that expense instead of passing it on to them."

Karen is focused on always growing as a leader and always looks for feedback where she needs to do better. "Superior communications skills are key to running the business and I never think I do as good a job as I can communicating to our employees. I see it as one of the areas of development we constantly have to address. Honestly. I communicate to my senior team a lot so they understand what I say and often what I'm thinking. I don't think the communication filters down the organization enough, and it's a challenge that we're aware of and we're addressing."

Lessons

"We try to see opportunities in everything we do. Even the loss of a respected colleague, as long as we learn from each of these events, I am okay with it. In terms of decision-making, I do take it down to a very basic concept. Now the guiding light for me, the thing that I do when I get all mucked up in my thoughts is to always step back and I say to myself, 'What's best for AGAR.' I go back and I ask myself that basic question."

"We had a top senior executive who became toxic to the organization. After a long and difficult effort we decided that this individual couldn't stay here, because we now focus on what's best for AGAR. He needed to leave. This way of working takes all the emotion out of it. Even though I personally struggle with losing somebody I care about, you still have to go back to basic survival instincts and be sure we're making decisions that are best for AGAR."

"We held this person to the same standard that we held everyone to. We gave him every chance in the world to change, and when he couldn't, he had to go. No double standard. You don't compromise the company for anyone, because it's about survival. If there's something that's breaking the chain, then I can't take care of the people and the company."

"After I got married, I fired this executive when I was six months pregnant and going on maternity leave. He had helped transition this business through the early part of the turn around process. Then he started reading his own press releases, stopped working hard, and started acting unprofessionally. It doesn't make a difference if it's the sweeper or an executive. I agonized over this for a long time, but in the end I let him go."

"I brought the leadership team together the day before and said, 'I need you all to step up to another level for me to do this because you all know it's the right thing.' Everybody was on board."

"I went on maternity leave and because we took the effort to build the right team, the results were great. We talked daily. I don't think I went into the office more than once in two months. They would call me if they had anything important to deal with. It was what I wanted. I don't want to be that important. I don't want AGAR to be Karen. I want AGAR to be the organization."

"I give my leadership team a lot of rope. For example, while I was on maternity leave, I trusted their decisions because I knew we were all in sync with what we were doing. I might not have done what they did in the same way, which is okay, but I didn't want them to feel I was questioning everything. On the other hand, I still see my role as the driver. Dad always said, 'Nothing happens unless you make it happen,' which I believe as well. I'm always trying to stir things up. I love it when people take things and run with them."

"Today the business is on a better footing, but I never take anything for granted and always work as if it can all go back in the tank again. I have had a leadership coach for years and more recently, I joined a CEO forum. It's a female CEO group and everyone's very candid. They say, 'Are you crazy, you did that?' This group is not timid. They are not afraid to say what they think, and they pig-pile on me. I realize I should listen to their perspective because these are very successful business people. Fortunately, we're all in totally different businesses. I try to be just a sponge off everyone."

Summary

Karen charged head first into the CEO role hoping that she could save the business and be an innovator. In the process she re-worked the company from top to bottom and built a strong balance sheet. She changed the culture from failure to a winning attitude and in the process changed people and the style of her management team. She said to them, 'I'm the leader, but you're leaders too.' She took tough and unpopular stands because once she found her guiding principle, "Do what's best for AGAR," she knew she had a model that applied to every situation. With that in her hip pocket she became a bolder version of herself. She taught her employees to see innovation as a badge of honor. We're AGAR, we're different, which is exactly what we want to be. We'll take risks that our competitors may not. And if it doesn't work out, we'll dust ourselves off and try something else. Karen learned to use the fact that she did not look or act like a traditional food industry executive to her advantage. Her independence, dignity, intellect, insight and emotional strength allowed her to stand up to insurmountable odds and say I don't have all the answers, so let me know what you think and then let's perform with distinction.

She taught her team that the same rules apply to all and that she expected them to hold themselves and everyone to these high standards. She established that good communication was an area that had to be constantly improved and that it could be a competitive advantage. And she held firm that being part of AGAR was a reward and that not everybody will fit with this team.

Karen defines the role of the 24-Hour leader as someone with true courage who was unafraid to face the issues, ask for help, and confidently to say, "I've made a decision, this is what we're going to do." As she had hoped, her vision and forthrightness has earned the admiration and respect of employees, colleagues, customers, government officials, peers, and family.

Author's 24-Hour Turnaround Score: 89

Karen's 24-Hour Leadership Rules:

∞ Leaders make tough decisions

∞ Leaders lead change. It's like the great athlete who wants the ball when the game is on the line

∞ Be the final decision maker, but don't hesitate to get support for making tough decisions

∞ Always strive to get better and learn on the job

∞ Be innovative despite what everyone else might be doing

∞ Build a team that is focused on the same goals

∞ Communication is essential

∞ Keep things simple

∞ Ask for help

∞ Communicate with customers, colleagues, and employees more than you think you should

Image 3: Karen and Grandpa Karl

Image 4: Karen and Dad on Sideline at Patriots Game Nov 2008

Image 5: Karen

4 From Humble Beginnings to a Market Leader

**Richard Cohen, CEO,
Classico Productions**
(http://www.classicoproductions.com)

The Company

Classico Productions, Aldenham, UK

"Let's Put on a Show and Make It Unforgettable."
This is the way of doing business at Classico
Productions, a seven-year-old event production
company whose CEO has more than twenty
years experience in the industry. They have the
capabilities to address the needs of both the
private and corporate sectors offering total
planning services to all clients. Their reputation
is built on the delivery of the very highest quality
of professionalism and expertise.

The CEO

Richard is proof that there is truth in the saying"
cream will always rise to the top." His story is one
of an unlikely entrepreneur who, due to his
customer orientation, respect for people, and
innate intelligence developed into an unlikely
24-Hour leader. Richard is a humble man who
had a secure job with a successful events
company that was prospering. Yet he knew
something was wrong with the way things were
being done and it gave him a restless feeling. It

was difficult for him when he realized that he was personally responsible for developing and preserving most of their business. He realized that if he left and started his own business in which he were calling the shots, the business would be much better and he would be happier as well. At the same time, most career employees do not typically venture out on their own without some episode and a lot of pre-planning and careful consideration. Richard knew there was job stability but little other upside in his current situation. He was also seeing aspects from the customer service perspective that he felt should be done better. Every day he saw flawed implementation, squandered opportunities and poor customer service.

"I had worked for my former company for eight years. I practically ran the entire events and production team. I had a fair salary and things were good. But the birth of my daughter made me wake up and smell the roses. I thought, 'I can do this by myself and can do a lot better.' At the time it was all about believing in me, about believing that people would actually want to use Richard Cohen to manage their event properly. So I had to take a real gamble. Within two months of starting the business, I had confirmed work of just over £120,000. So it was quite amazing. My business strategy was simple. I contacted people I had been working with at my previous company, and as they knew me, they were extremely happy to do business with me."

"I went from earning an average salary at the former company to running an £1.1 million business in my first year. So financially, I didn't know what hit me. I had to take some actions very quickly. It never occurred to me that I would have to make financial plans. But I soon discovered that we needed a tight cash-flow system. Today, I know what goes in and I know what goes out. I know how much money's in the business at any one time. We never overstep ourselves, which is why a lot of my competitors have fallen over in the last six months and why we're thriving."

"Looking back now, I realize that I had no real business aspirations, dreams, or prospects of opening my own business. My first real job was as a DJ, which I enjoyed. But as I saw my friends and colleagues going on to become doctors and lawyers, I wondered where being a DJ was going to lead me." Even further from his thoughts was the idea that he would one day leave that company to start his own business and build a top-of-the-line enterprise based on hard work, creativity, dedication to quality, and a team of very committed people.

With Richard it all started at home: "I did not come from a family of entrepreneurs. I have a modest background. I was extremely insecure as a child especially about my weight. My dad went to work for my mom's dad, and ran a menswear shop in London for 25 years. He sold that business and then ran a jewelry business for two years. Then he came to work for me. He is now retired. My mom, through sheer hard work and determination, started off as a temp for Deutsche Bank and 30 years later she's now vice president of the legal department. I don't think that's entrepreneurial, but I think I get my true grit and determination from my mom. My mom was a big influence on setting up the business. I would go to her for legal advice, because I knew that what she was offering me was always correct."

Company's History

"We are an event management and production company. We're actually a one-stop shop. So either a hotel, a private client, or a corporate client can come to Classico Productions for the entire event package. We will coordinate and organize the venue. What makes it very different from other companies is that everything is done in-house. Over the last seven years the main focus of the company has been making sure that we own all our equipment. We don't want to outsource, because the moment we outsource we reduce our quality and profit margin. We spent the first three years of business buying the equipment. It was so important for us to build a sizeable inventory. Today, when things are tough, every job that we do is a profitable job, because we've eliminated equipment leasing costs. We have the ability to make a substantial profit on the job because of all the investments that we've made over the last few years. The client can come to us for absolutely everything. We are currently working on an event in a hotel where we're providing all the exhibition stands. We're planning a party for a Greek airline in one of the top hotels in London where we're doing all the creative production for them. Every event that we do and every concept we create is unique and different. Over the last few years we have built up the reputation that our company can do anything. It gained momentum because people believed in me."

Getting Started

Classico Productions serves a high-end London clientele, which is a sophisticated and incredibly demanding group. When Richard targeted this audience he knew that even though he was starting with nothing, he would have to project the image of a top-notch operation.

Richard constantly learned by doing. "I started Classico Productions with zero. I had zero money in my bank account. In fact, I was actually £40,000 in debt when I started my business. When I set up my business bank account the bank manager asked me how much I was putting in. To my embarrassment I simply replied "I haven't got anything." "Within two weeks I was able to put £19,000 in my bank account, which was a deposit I received from a forthcoming event. That's how I built the business up. I had to learn on the job about financial planning. I wanted to learn all the logistics of this business more than anything. And that's what I've done. I think it is because I did it myself that the whole business runs so smoothly now. One amazing thing is that we have never had to create a mission statement...Everyone who is employed by Classico knows what we are doing and why. In seven years of being in business, we have never done a day's advertising or any marketing. Our business has been built by word of mouth."

"I also hired and took the advice of an accountant who has worked with me for the last several years. I have come to appreciate that if you don't have good professional advisors from day one, your business may not succeed."

Problems and Challenges

"I am a very spiritual person. I believe that whatever happens in life, it happens for a reason. At the time I set up the business, I was in the right place, at the right time, in an economy that was thriving. Seven years down the line, I know where I came from, I know who I am, and I have the self-belief that I can actually do anything that I put my mind to. It's all about being positive, staying positive, and respecting everybody who works around you. It is not just about business. I bring my personal life into my business life, and the two things work together.

In the end it was believing in myself and wanting it. It was having the will to succeed and also the ability to accept support at those times when people said I couldn't do it."

"The challenges are different now. When I worked for someone else I had to deal with their values and processes and when they did something poorly I was often the one to clean up the mess. As the business owner, everything that happens in the business now rests on my shoulders."

"I am currently working on events that I never dreamed possible or ever imagined that people would hire me for. These included providing sound and lighting for concerts and providing large conference stage sets for major blue chip companies. Every job we do now is an exciting challenge. Our successes truly come down to:

1. Great organization in planning the event
2. Having the experience and knowing that what we are providing is going to succeed
3. Believing in our own abilities

"Part of success in the event planning business, like anything else, is knowing when to say 'no,' as interesting and lucrative as that work may be. I was in that situation a couple of years ago. We were offered an opportunity to work with a multinational corporation which, at the time, was an amazing opportunity for my company. We really were excited. They asked us to undertake the sponsorship management, which in effect is carrying out the actual marketing of the event. I have no experience in sponsorship management. So after being offered a six-figure contract I had to turn it down. It didn't play to our strengths."

Strategies and Action Steps

Quality Defines the Strategy

"A phrase we use to describe our work is 'Creating Hallmark Events.' We believe the word hallmark really does make a statement about creativity and quality. We are at the very high-end of the market, and I think the word hallmark says top quality. It implies excellence. In the beginning the business was just me. At that time, everything had to be outsourced. I decided to take on my first employee, a disc jockey after six months. I purchased, for the business, just about £12,000 worth of DJ equipment so that we didn't have to outsource it. The biggest problem was that we didn't have anywhere to store it. For the following six months we had a massive amount of equipment living in my dining room, which didn't make my wife too happy. Somewhat by accident, this strategy became a cornerstone of the business, that is, re-invest and buy, don't outsource equipment. By following that principle, even when we had very little money, we were able to control the profits of the business."

"We did a job for a big hotel group where we installed a tennis court in the venue. Profit from the event allowed us to buy over £50,000 of equipment. The only problem was that we had no way to store it, and so we transformed my garage into a bit more of a warehouse type space, but it just did not work. We then got very lucky. I had a friend who owned a warehouse. I offered him £200 for a little corner in his warehouse. He said to me, '£200, don't insult me, you can have it for nothing.' I did that. I took it for nothing." True to his humble personality, what Richard likes to call luck is really his ability to see and seize opportunities.

"I was taking my oldest daughter for a bike ride, and noticed that there were these fantastic barns. I just happened to bump into one of the farmers there and said, 'I don't suppose I can hire one of these?' Within a month we had transformed a 2,500-square-foot barn into a 2,500-square-foot working warehouse. We are in the process now of building offices and additional workable space so that the whole business can be run from this location. So it's those kinds of fortuitous events that have allowed the business to thrive."

"A business relationship is like a love affair. The relationship needs to be carefully nurtured in good and bad times. Even now, in tough times, the relationships I had leading up to the recession are still going strong because these companies trust us and know we are going to deliver exactly what they need."

Leadership Style

"Leadership is all about how to talk to people. This business runs successfully because I have total respect for my staff. There's always been that amazing relationship that I've had with them. [In past jobs] I was screamed and shouted at and told I was useless, and that I couldn't do a job properly, even if I tried. To me, that is no way to look after your employees. I also believe that leadership is about how you treat your suppliers. It's about how to talk to them and how you pay them. With other companies, suppliers have to wait 90 or 120 days for something that they've already worked on. Every single one of my suppliers, especially when I first started the business, was paid within fourteen to thirty days."

Richard thinks of himself as a decent and fair person and those are the qualities he looks for in all the people he hires."I hire people who possess special character. I look for approachable, caring people. I don't want someone coming in here thinking that they know better than anybody else. I want staff who can learn. An excellent example is an employee we hired straight out of college as an assistant to an events director. Over the last two and a half years, she performed so well that when the events director left, I didn't hesitate in giving her that role."

"When hiring a new employee, I'm looking for people who have self-belief. I look for people who know they can do the job and want to succeed in this business, as much as I wanted to. Everyone who works here has a defined role. If they do their jobs and they do them well, then they tend to be happy here. If they don't, they don't work for me. It's as simple as that."

"It is absolutely all about the character of the person. They're not hard-nosed. They're personable and customer-oriented. I think people warm to this kind of personality. I am as soft as they come. I actually think that's more endearing than somebody whose emotions are hard to read. I want to know how people feel. I think that comes across really well. I think when you sell and people see you as being honest, as being the genuine article, it helps. I would much rather people say to me, 'Richard, you are so lovely to deal with, you did such an amazing job,' as opposed to someone saying, 'He did a great job, but what an asshole.' There are so many people that are like that. They are the ones who are struggling at the moment."

Richard learned important lessons from his former company. He watched them doing events in a way that he considered flawed. He saw the way they treated employees, customers, and suppliers and he noted that if he had the chance he would do things differently.

"I always try to do right by my people. I have never, in seven years of being in business, screamed at any of my staff. I have rarely fired anybody. We've kept much of the same staff for the whole seven years. They want the business and me to be successful and they want to share in that success as well. It's that sort of attitude that has taken us to where we are within the industry and we're in a fantastic place. We work seven days a week, so there's never a close down. As a result, you've got to be able to find the balance between constantly working and being with your family. If somebody has a personal issue in the office with regard to their family, then I'll send them home. Family is more important than work."

Message and Lessons

Richard believes it is important to put your personal baggage behind you. "What shaped me more than anything else is believing in myself and knowing I can do it. That means ignoring the demons and insecurities from the past, and then going forward. I was given an opportunity. I should say I created the opportunity because I believed that it was something I could do and there was room in the industry for me. Now I look back on those years and I can't believe I'm the same person. That's what I find amazing. When I compare who I was ten or fifteen years ago to who I am today, with regard to my thinking and my attitude, my whole concept of life has changed so much. I trust in myself and I do the right thing in my business as well as my personal life."

24-Hour Leaders find their own leadership voice and create balance in their life to follow their dreams and pursue the things they believe in. For Richard, finding his voice was connected with gaining personal self-confidence. He listened to the people around him and advisors that supported him and were convinced he would do well.

"I looked to my mom, my wife, and my employees, who are mostly women. I have an abundance of people that I can talk to at any time. I'm very open in the office. I'm very open with everybody. Everyone here knows the state of the business, where the business is, where the business is heading. I involve everybody in the decision-making, but of course, I make the final decision."

"I know I make mistakes and I think a lot about how I treat people, especially when something goes wrong. When you do wrong by people, then you've got to have enough courage to turn around and say, 'I'm sorry, I made a mistake on that.' And put your hand up and say, 'It won't happen again.' None of us is perfect. In business you do make mistakes. I've made plenty. I'm the first to admit it. However, I've learned from every mistake I've made. It's a learning curve."

"Every day, when I get out of bed, I am excited because you never know what great thing could happen today. When I woke up this morning, I had no idea that I was going to come into work and there was going to be a contract on my desk from a hotel in London to say that we're doing a £10,000-event for them this weekend."

"I was offered a piece of advice that I've taken with me for the past few years. My business coach said to me that I've got to believe in myself. He also encouraged me to take chances and I thought, if I don't take these chances now, I'm not going to make it. From the day I met my business coach, I believed in him. There was something about him that said to me that he saw me as having that intangible to be an extraordinarily successful entrepreneur and he wanted to help me get there. I think that's really nice."

"As I said before, early in my work life I was a DJ, and I am now running a complex set of specialty business projects for extremely demanding clients. These are clients who want the latest technology delivered flawlessly, on time and on budget. I had to learn all aspects of running my own business. I learned by watching and by doing. I don't spend a lot of time talking to my employees about integrity because I believe in teaching by acting with integrity."

Richard also believes that in his company, everyone strives for perfection. "I know this sounds ridiculous, but people rarely do anything wrong here because they all have such a great understanding of the work. We are all on the same path. We are all trying to achieve the same thing, which tends to minimize mistakes."

He is also not afraid to make tough people decisions. "I think of myself as a nice person, but I am not afraid to make the tough decisions. I had to make a decision to fire somebody a few years ago. This was a woman who came to work for me nine months after setting up the business. She brought in many contracts with blue chip companies. These resulted in a substantial amount of business for us. Due to other behaviors I couldn't continue a working relationship with her, and I had to make a decision to let her go. It was probably one of the best decisions I made, because three years after that we've now set up a secondary business between the two of us, which we turned into a corporate events company, and it's set up to be quite successful. So it's strange how it all comes about. I think that was probably one of the hardest decisions I made, but in the end it worked out well for both of us."

For Richard, it wasn't easy to trust people to do things exactly the way he would.

"I used to do everything. I used to have to do everything myself. Today I've got a lot more trust in people who work with me. I actually let go of some aspects of the business and just rely on the fact that my staff can do it. I've never been let down. So from that sense, everyone knows what jobs they've got to do and everyone gets on with it. And if mistakes are made, I always know about it because I'm so involved in the business."

Richard is also a firm believer that giving back is good business. "I have done charity jobs for as many as 600 people, where we've sponsored and paid for the entire event. I sponsored a young girl who had a serious illness. A year after her chemotherapy, we created an incredible party for her and 120 of her friends and family. It was all sponsored by Classico Productions. We had an amazing evening. Doing these things not only makes all of us feel good, but it also helps define who we are to the public.

Summary

The conventional wisdom is that humble, nice, thoughtful people cannot survive in highly competitive industries. Richard Cohen proves conventional wisdom wrong. Richard started out at about the lowest role one could have as his first job, by his own description, "I literally started right at the bottom, just DJ-ing for the company, if you excuse the expression, schlepping the equipment, and lots of labor-intensive work." At that point even he would not have predicted the path he would follow. This sensitive man was driven to pursue a career in an industry known for unrelenting competition and figured out a way to not only thrive but to rise to the top. He will tell you that his business plan is in his head and if you confuse that with meaning he doesn't have a plan, you have underestimated Richard. He knows everything that's going on at all times. He says his employees rarely make mistakes. That is not by chance. It is the result of mutual affection and a mutually deep commitment to a business that demands nothing less than perfection. Why has Richard retained so many of his customers when his competitors are struggling to do as well in tough economic times? His magic is that his customers are as loyal to him as are his employees. They come back to him for a very simple reason. They know how much he cares about them and is never happy with anything less than a spectacular event.

Author's 24-Hour Turnaround Score: 90

Richard's 24-Hour Leadership Principles:

∞ Find your own voice, follow your dreams, and pursue the things you believe in

∞ A business relationship is like a love affair

∞ Learn by doing

∞ Quality defines the strategy

∞ Leadership is about communication and respect

∞ Be relentless in providing quality and satisfaction to everything you do

∞ Hire people who possess special character

∞ Being genuine is key

∞ Always do right by your people

∞ Manage your demons and put your personal baggage behind you

∞ Do not be scared to make tough people-decisions

Image 6: A Classico Event

Figure 7: Another Classico Event

Image 8: Richard the Shining Star Behind the Party

Chapter 4: From Humble Beginnings to a Market Leader

5 Driven by Diligence, Loyalty, and Rewarding Excellence

Ken Ferry, CEO, iCAD, Inc.
(http://WWW.ICADMED.COM)

The Company

iCAD, Inc. (NASDAQ: ICAD) is an industry-leading provider of advanced image analysis and workflow software solutions. These tools enable healthcare professionals to serve patients better by identifying pathologies and pinpointing cancer earlier than traditional methods. Since receiving FDA approval for the company's first breast cancer detection product in 2002, over 3,100 iCAD systems have been placed in healthcare practices worldwide. iCAD's solutions aid in the early detection of the most prevalent cancers including breast, colon, prostate and in the future, lung cancer.

The CEO: Measurement Is Key and Everyone Counts

Ken Ferry leveraged a very successful career at a multinational medical products giant to become the CEO of a smaller but high-potential medical software company called iCAD. His previous experience had clearly demonstrated his ability to lead unprecedented growth. He was the senior vice president and general manager for the Global Patient Monitoring business for Philips

Medical Systems, the market leader in a $2.5 billion industry. In 2001, he also became the senior vice president for the parent company, Philips Electronics Medical Systems Division.

"At Philips I had the benefit of running the field organization first for six or seven years. So when I flipped to the general management side, running the field gave me extremely good insight. That's something a lot of people don't do. They either come up through the technology side of the business or they're in sales or marketing and somehow the board believes that a sales person is the right fit to run a company. I had the unique opportunity of having both the general management and field sides, which gave me tremendous experience and perspective because I could relate to all aspects of the business."

Throughout his career, Ken has been recognized as a business leader and motivator. He understands what makes teams successful. He drives discipline and focuses on winning and made it easily to our list of 24-Hour Leaders.

iCAD's History

iCAD was founded in 1984 by an optical engineer as a digitizer business. Digitizing means converting standard analog images into digital content. At the start, they were selling to a variety of industries, with healthcare being just one of many markets. In healthcare, digitizers were primarily used to take X-rays and turn them into digital images. At that point the company was equally focused on selling to the graphic arts industry and every place else that used this technology. Some time before Ken got there, they decided to focus on a vertical channel strategy. To implement this plan they made two acquisitions of companies that made CAD (Computer-Aided Detection) software. One was in Beaver Creek, OH, and one was in Tampa, FL. The Florida acquisition was folded into Ohio and the company was organized around two sites, research and development in Beaver Creek, OH, and headquarters in Nashua, NH.

"Since I came on board we've changed the value proposition. In the past they would say we're a CAD company and we find breast cancer. Now we say, 'We're in the image analysis and workflow business. Our focus is on the most prevalent cancers, which is breast, lung, colorectal, and prostate.'"

"From a business standpoint, in the beginning, what got me interested in iCAD was the potential to build a $200 million business after we fixed the existing $20 million business, which was not performing up to expectations. That's the kind of stuff that gets you excited. This business is diverse enough that you can get your competitive and intellectual juices flowing. You can really accomplish something significant that serves people with life-threatening diseases. And, if you do it right, you can make some money."

Strategic growth was key for Ken. "We use the most common imaging technologies to detect, diagnose, or assess if a treatment is doing what it's supposed to do. We're in the image analysis and workflow business. To grow the business we're taking a combined organic (internal growth) and an inorganic (acquisition) approach. We recently bought a small company out of White Plains, NY that has CAD for MRI. They had two approved products, one for breast and one for prostate."

"We are constantly on the move as it relates to acquisitions. We've made one, and we have looked at a lot of others. We haven't done anything else yet, but we intend to. Our strategy is clear to my direct staff. The challenge is, from an employee communications standpoint, we need to improve the dissemination of that message so that everybody in the company is clear on what we're trying to accomplish. We're constantly working on improving company-wide communication and are getting better at it."

Challenges and Problems

iCAD was a good company that had stalled. For the company to get on the right track again it needed to find senior staff and a talented sales force. "The organization needed to get focused around an aggressive set of goals or they would not grow and could even eventually fail."

Ken had a track record of successfully building large organizations. His entry into iCAD would test his experience and strategies because now he was in a much smaller organization that was missing big pieces of infrastructure and key personnel. Could he achieve the stated iCAD goal of advancing from $20 to $200 million? Ken worked first to understand the issues. The question was: Could he overcome the obstacles he was facing quickly enough to turn things around on time?

Ken was confident that he could succeed. "I have strong domain knowledge in medical devices and felt this would be an advantage in moving ahead. I knew I had to change the culture and thought about how I was going to change the fragmented culture into one that demanded excellence. I worked to put the right management team in place."

Ken's turnaround plan was to show people though his actions rather than just words. "I made my presence felt by being very visible throughout the company. Right away this distinguished me from the previous management. I constantly articulated the vision and goals, and made it clear to everyone what their roles and responsibilities were. I knew that our ability to stick to that plan was the key to iCAD's success."

As he describes it, "You do think you know a lot. If you're at a senior level, you've been around a lot of years you think you know everything, and then you go into a small business or a different business and you learn how much you can learn and it just stimulates you again. I've learned a lot and had to put more emphasis on financial metrics that I never used to worry about, like cash flow."

"In a small business you learn real fast what expenses sit in your income statement that are cash-related, and what are expenses related to accounting, meaning that expenses which are not related to cash aren't nearly as important as those that are."

While Ken is teaching himself about iCAD's financial-drivers, he's also focusing on the fact that he took over an organization that was missing a strong sense of purpose. "I knew that I had a relatively short time to turn things around." The plan was simple:

1. Develop a vision and get people to believe in it
2. Get the right people in place with the right skills and mindset

3. Bring all employees together around a common set of goals
4. Understand the financial drivers of this business
5. Drive discipline and accountability so that employees deliver what they promise
6. Reward employees for their contributions
7. Transition the prior team out while launching the new team with a minimal loss of momentum

Importance of Being Visible

"When I took the job, the first thing I did was ask if they ever had an all-company meeting with R&D and headquarters, all in one site. They had never done it. There were a number of people who never even met each other. They talked on the phone, but never met. So I said we're going to have a meeting in Ohio, not Nashua, because that's where I thought the hotspot of discontent would be. I went out to Ohio for two days and we had a very strong, positive meeting. For the first year I would go out there twice a month. I was there almost as much as I was at the headquarters. It was important to show up. My staff meetings were always in Ohio. It got people on board and believing in the strategy. They were becoming confident about what we could do."

Another key to success was upgrading the executive talent and building a circle of close, trusted colleagues: "I brought Stacey Stevens and Jeff Barnes, both former colleagues from Philips, in to run strategy, marketing, and sales. They had worked for me in a number of different capacities in the past, but this was different. I said I might be the band leader here, but we're like peers. We're doing this together. We're like a three-person turnaround team. I wasn't trying to re-create the old Philips group, but I wanted people I knew in critical roles. To bring in new talent, I used a search firm to find a CFO and head of R&D from outside. The CFO we hired had that role at three public companies in the past. She filled an important gap because of her experience in talking to investors and analysts. I wanted a CFO who had raised money and done deals. I wanted someone who had talked to investors and knew that whole process."

"The other key position was the head of R&D who also came from outside. Our product is based on radiologist workflow. The last thing I wanted was the head of R&D to be a person with a very narrow technology background. The person I hired came from a PACS (Picture Archiving and Communication Systems) company. PACS are all about workflow. Unfortunately, that hire caused disappointment and resignations. We had two critical R&D people leave the company within 90 days of when I hired the new R&D head."

With the level of organizational changes going on Ken needed to do several things quickly: "I needed to reassure the remaining organization so no one else would leave. I also needed some quick wins, so people would believe in the future of the company. The employees needed to see an accessible CEO and a management team that was talented and worked well together, and finally an aggressive business plan that they believed could stabilize things and grow the company."

Ken used his strong financial background to deal with the pressures of a small company. "You have to expense stock options. We expense maybe three-quarters of a million a quarter. It's all non-cash, so it affects your earnings per share but it doesn't affect your cash flow. It's an accounting exercise, like depreciation. These are things you never think about in a big company, such as cash, receivables, how much cash we brought in this month, or how much cash we burned? Here you have tremendous highs and lows compared to a large company that is more stable."

"At HP or Philips there was almost always a cushion. It was not uncommon to have a backlog where I could almost dial in my next quarter because I had six to twelve weeks of backlog. At iCAD, 75 percent of the business is booked and shipped in the same quarter. So backlog has far less meaning. It can add a lot of stress to your life because you don't know what's going to happen."

Strategies and Action Steps

Running a small company was a new experience, especially when I had spent my career up to now dealing with bigger organizations. Having a plan and delivering on that plan became that much more important. "At the start, bringing in people I knew was the most important step. iCAD had really good technology but it was not a strong organization and they had a poor sales and marketing team. My strategy was to take on the weakest link first. The technology was great, which is so important in an FDA-regulated business. Fixing technology could take years to improve it. But fixing sales and marketing is something you can do a lot faster."

"It was disruptive to bring in new people, but it was survival. In the second quarter of 2006 we did $3.8 million in revenue and lost $2.5 million. That was 20 percent negative growth over the prior quarter." With the financials going in the wrong direction, Ken needed to be sure he had the backing of the chairman and the board. "I learned through my own due diligence [prior to joining] that the chairman was very credible in saying that I would get the time and get a long enough runway to turn things around, which is what we did. We were able to do it because I knew I had the chairman's trust and that he would give us a reasonable chance to succeed."

The key for Ken was to continually adapt his leadership style to the circumstances that were going on as the company tried to progress. Ken's drive to succeed was always clear as was the level of integrity he brought to everything he did. "I think integrity and doing things honestly and still being the best is as good as it gets." You have to have personal integrity. You also have to empower others and demonstrate the trust you have in them. For example, one of the biggest challenges you have in a small company is revenue recognition and there's a lot of pressure there. I said to the new CFO, 'You're in charge of revenue recognition. Don't even ask me, because you're the one who needs to sign all the financial statements at the end of the quarter. If an order comes in and we ship it and the terms are not consistent with good revenue recognition policy, I want you to be the final authority, not me. You're the one who makes those decisions.'"

"Things have worked out well with the new leadership team. The people I brought in from Philips have blended well with the new members. It works because we've put a team together who are of high intellect, they have complementary skills, and they're able to work together to get things done. They're also fun people who I enjoy having dinner and a bottle of wine with."

Ken had to be decisive and act quickly: "I had to force out 75 percent of the board I inherited. Some of them went absolutely kicking and screaming because we were starting to turn the business around, the stock was starting to move up, and they didn't want to leave."

"I wanted smart people on the board. I recruited Tony Ecock from a private equity firm in New York City. At Philips Tony was my predecessor in running the global patient monitoring business and I was running sales and marketing. We were peers. I recruited him because I wanted someone on the board who had been in my shoes. I wanted someone I felt comfortable asking tough questions, who had good intuition, and understood the need to adapt to the situations we were facing. It was really great having all the pieces move into place. It's fun now. I had the staff and the board I needed."

"When I first took over, I recognized many of the problems at iCAD, but I didn't know all the fixes. Some things were easy to resolve. For example, the company was missing medical device industry domain knowledge from their CEO. The former CEO was really a general counsel, with no healthcare background. That was part of the situation they brought me in here to fix. Other, more complex problems, like building a unified organization across two sites, took more time and required a high level of cooperation from the board, my staff, and the rest of the company. Therefore, having the right people in place quickly at all levels was critical."

Organizational Philosophy

Employee development was a priority for Ken in building the business: "I'm a big supporter of a practical, pragmatic approach to employee development. I like development that makes sense for the individual, not the one where I say, 'These are your weaknesses, and you need to go and take a course.' Even though giving tough feedback can be difficult, I think it's important to have candid discussions about skills and weaknesses, particularly interpersonal skills. For example, in the past I said to an employee, 'You can be a bull in a china shop. I've seen and also gotten feedback that you don't listen carefully and often interrupt people when we're at meetings.' I don't think classes are usually the answer for improving interpersonal skills. I'd rather set goals for their improvement and help coach them through it than to send them off to some executive training for them to try to figure it out."

"My job is to give employees feedback. I don't do performance evaluations [with the senior managers]. I do a written quarterly review with them. Each staff member sits down with me and says, 'Here are my performance objectives.' We discuss them, we agree on an updated plan and they go off and do them. I try to let people know that their hard work is recognized and appreciated. I need to ensure that everyone on the team knows what was expected of them. At the end of a quarter, we have a one hour, one-on-one individually based dashboard goals and performance summary they fill out. We talk about their performance against those objectives. We discuss it and I give them feedback on that, and then we agree on next quarter's objectives. That's it."

Communication and Meetings

"In a small company people know what's going on. We don't need staff meetings. If I need to talk about an issue, I figure out which people need to be involved in it and we have a meeting or we have a phone call. We used to have more formal meetings, but it wasn't productive. It was mostly a parade of PowerPoint presentations that didn't move us forward. It's not a question of staff meetings or no staff meetings. It boils down to what's required for people to have the information they need to be able to act independently and make good decisions."

"Everyone is moving in the same direction now, which is a huge change. And we're all in agreement on what good performance is all about. When I first got here, we had a sales force that couldn't stand up and make a polished presentation. They would bring up a little cheat sheet and half of them showed up late, which was never going to happen again."

"I did get a lot of help from my brother, who was the CEO of several public companies. He's a great backstop for me to bounce things off of. He told me something when I first became CEO, which I thought was extraordinary. He said, 'The first person that would like to buy your stock is me, but I'm not going to buy a share, because if I'm not a shareholder then we can talk about anything you want at any time.'"

Celebrating Accomplishments

"We like to celebrate our successes. At the end of a recent quarter, even though the quarter was tough because of the economy, we still broke out champagne once we finished shipping and booking. We have the operations team here including manufacturing, order processing, credit, and collections who bust their backs at the end of the quarter. When the dust is all settled by 5:05 [p.m.] on the last day, we always break out champagne and sit around and celebrate, even if it's not a great quarter. We do it to recognize people's efforts."

Ken also believes that rewarding people financially is also a key to success. "Personal success is a blend of people's success and financial success. There's this old expression: Your job as a leader is to grow the business and to grow the people. I look at both as equally important. I take a lot of pride out of seeing people develop and get better at what they do. For example, 2007 was something of a breakthrough. It was our first full year here, and we took the business into cash flow positive range Things were going well. For my staff we had a bonus scheme that tied bonuses to accomplishments and we blew it away. The bonus scheme allowed us to pay a maximum of 200 percent of the bonus target. We had this great year and exceeded those goals. I was so impressed with what we did I went to the board and I said, 'I want to pay out above their bonus targets. In addition, I want to give everybody on the executive staff the same percentage—not the same bonus, but the same percentage of their base to reinforce the fact that we did it as a team."

Ken is also a leader who believes that actions speak louder than words. As objectives changed Ken decided to change the bonus strategy in year two. "In my first year I felt that paying the leadership team's bonuses at an equal percentage sent a critical message that would support the value of pulling together as a team in the right direction. In the second year I felt I could now start to distinguish performance better in some cases than others. In my second year, bonuses were based on performance in some priority order. Not everybody agreed with my assessment, but I had a discussion with every person and told them exactly how I assessed their performance, what they earned, and why. It wasn't a huge difference, but there were differences, and I was clear about what my thinking was in each case."

Ken's values and style have been consistent throughout his management career. He benefitted from working for good companies like Hewlett-Packard, which had a corporate philosophy that balanced the needs of the company with the needs of its employees. In the end, management style is a reflection of business goals combined with personal values and experiences.

"I think it starts with family. My parents both did not get high school diplomas. My father was an electrician and my mom was a homemaker, but they established great values. They were great examples as a couple. They were hard working people who would mortgage everything they had to make sure their three sons got really good college educations. They made big sacrifices because they believed in the benefits of a good education. I can't pinpoint a particular event, but having the backstop of a good family and knowing that if I wanted to do something risky I had a lot of support behind me made all the difference in the world. It probably made moving up into senior leadership roles easier to do because I knew I had the proper support and family to back me up if I ran into problems."

Lessons

Key to building success was in focusing on values and attracting new staff with values. "You've got your principles as to how you run a business. You have to change your behavior or change how you do things sometimes. But you don't want to compromise your values. You don't change your beliefs about how you want to run your business. This balance of values and day-to-day decisions gets constantly challenged in a small company. You tend to be more responsive to crises and tactical issues than in a big company because in big companies there are layers of people dealing with every issue. Just by virtue of size, the values of a small company tend to be more obvious. We want to create an environment that attracts top people. We want to attract people who are extremely smart, well educated, very strong, and capable. We want people who fit well with this culture. At a company like iCAD, employees are not burdened with working through layers of process, infrastructure, policy, and levels of approval that you'd find in a big organization. They're just getting things done, which means they're typically more self-reliant and more accountable than their big-company counterparts. We need people who are adaptable and at the same time committed to a high-performance culture. As you look at this environment, what you find is that the people are of an incredibly high caliber."

"Leading a public company like this one is a little different than what I have experienced before. You've got people who move with great urgency. They have to get things done fast. Bureaucratic corporations didn't have to move at that pace. I'm trying to create a real high-performance culture, high-integrity, high-quality, but no short cuts. I'm also saying, 'Cut through the garbage, let's get the job done. Feel empowered, make decisions, and don't feel like everything has to fall back into your boss's lap. We can't be a big hierarchical structure.' In this environment, within reason, I make the rules. If I decide the rules are that you're empowered to make decisions, as long as you're responsible about it, we'll support you whether it's a good or bad decision."

Surprisingly, fear can help. "You have to have confidence in yourself. You have to have the right approach from a business-fundamental standpoint. Having said that, it may seem weird, but you have to fear failing. It's the people who are most cocky and confident who are most likely to get blindsided. It actually helps to have that moment about once or twice a week when you say, 'Did I really make the right decision? Was this the right approach? Did I make a mistake or am I or the company at risk of failing.' It's not even second-guessing as much as you should fear that you could fail."

Acknowledgement for Success Well Earned

"October is breast cancer awareness month. We were invited to ring the closing bell at NASDAQ in October. This is probably one of the most exciting moments we have had as a company. I brought twenty-five people from iCAD to New York City. Then we went to the Marriott in Times Square and had a big party for everyone. NASDAQ does a phenomenal job on this stuff. They are very good at promotion.

That was such an incredible moment. I had my wife and my daughters there with me. We brought a lot of our key personnel. It was a great day in the market and the stock went up that day."

"I was also asked to appear on Fox Business News that evening. They were getting CEOs from all different industries—casinos, fast food, and others—and they were trying to understand what a bad economy was doing to our businesses and our ability to raise capital. It was a great experience. I was also interviewed the next day by different media and then had an interview with NASDAQ. It was an incredibly defining moment. It was the point where we could celebrate what we had become and the success we had achieved."

Summary

Ken is a professional executive who had risen to the top ranks of corporate America. When iCAD came calling he was ready for the challenges of leadership, but he found himself tackling bigger problems than he had seen in the past and wound up fighting for business survival. Ken's success is based on his knowing his own strengths and surrounding himself with trusted advisors and talented staff who could accept his leadership and move forward with authority. Ken leads by example and does not ask anyone to do something that he himself would not do. He practices sound business skills starting with a clear and accepted vision, quickly turning the vision into a working plan. Ken has the business acumen to communicate what's important and consistently demands excellence around execution of those principles. Ken relies heavily on numbers, and also understands people and what motivates them. He never loses sight of the goal and is generous in rewarding the team that ensures that the company reaches its lofty goals.

Author's 24-Hour Turnaround Score: 90

Ken's 24-Hour Leadership Principles:

∞ Be decisive and act quickly—don't look back—actions speak louder than words

∞ Work with a Board that will help you succeed

∞ Have trusted colleagues and advisors

∞ Having a vision, a plan and delivering on that plan equals success

∞ Know all the financial drivers of your business

∞ Leaders are visible and accessible

∞ Leaders are good teachers and understand staff development

∞ Communication is key

∞ Share the rewards—recognize, good performance and business success

∞ Adapt quickly to each new situation

Image 9: iCAD Team at Times Square

Image 10: iCAD Team—Closing Bell at NASDAQ

Chapter 5: Driven by Diligence, Loyalty, and Rewarding Excellence

6 From Star Struck to Entrepreneurial Star

Joel Rabinowitz, CEO, The House
joel.rabinowitz@yahoo.com

Se·ri·al en·tre·pre·neur, n: A serial entrepreneur starts several businesses within a lifetime, treating entrepreneurship as a profession rather than an occasional episode.

Five minutes with Joel and you know he is a born entertainer and entrepreneur. Joel is the story of a man who, from the time he was a little boy, knew what he was passionate about. In a world of short attention spans and interests that are revised hourly, Joel has stayed true to who he is. He follows his passions and turns them into successful enterprises again and again and again, but like everything with Joel there is a twist. He's built organizations, but his passion is making deals and amazingly he also makes friends along the way. Joel is a master at pushing through adversity and structuring deals built on friendship and trust. And he does this in the entertainment industry, where trust is a rare commodity.

"It all started with five words that changed my life forever. In February 1964, Ed Sullivan said, 'Ladies and gentlemen, the Beatles!' From that point on everything in the life of Joel Rabinowitz, a young kid from Montreal, Canada, and the son of a Holocaust survivor, was about to turn upside down. Who could have possibly known that after seeing the Beatles, Joel would go on a lifelong Magical Mystery Tour that would lead him into the world of entertainment, friendships with stars, and multiple business ventures.

"When I was 7, I had a little black and white TV set in my bedroom. I think eight o'clock was my bedtime, but occasionally we were allowed to stay up and watch the Ed Sullivan show. That night I was already half asleep and my mom came running up the stairs and said, 'Turn on the TV set! You won't believe what you're seeing!' I turned it on, and it was the Beatles playing 'All My Loving,' and 'Please, Please Me,' and at that moment my life changed instantly. I wanted to be Ringo Starr. I wanted to be a drummer in a rock and roll band. My dream for all those years was to sit behind Paul, John, and George. I would be bashing out the skins to those guys. What is amazing is that I eventually became friends with Ringo and I actually told him that story, which was embarrassing to do. I also told him that all my friends dreamed of being hockey *stars*. I wanted to be Ringo *Starr*. That was my line. Ringo thought it was pretty funny, too."

The Companies

In the beginning, Joel never thought of himself as a businessman. He was a kid who was passionate about music. So, since he had to work, working in the music business was a natural progression. But Joel had a knack for business and used his natural skills to become an entertaining 24-Hour leader. He was gregarious, hard-working, ambitious, personable, and responsible. Joel stood out! He eventually made friends and contacts that enabled him to turn his passion into a business. In fact, many businesses. He has lived through the booms and busts of entrepreneurship. Through all of this, he keeps his head up and presses on. All of this has allowed him to build a strong reputation and a 35-year track record as a successful entrepreneur.

First Job: Record Store Manager/District Manager

"This hot DJ, Earl Jive, did a radio show in Montreal, where I would bring my Beatle unreleased records. I had hundreds of them. We would listen with other DJs At that time I was working in a record store that specialized in bootleg albums, so I would scoop up all the Beatle albums and bring them right home and rush to the turntable and listen to them. I had a number of jobs in music stores. I was a manager of a record store and did very well. Then I got hired to become branch manager of a record company in Ontario."

"I was young and had success in the record store business. I also realized that this was not going to be where I was going to stay my whole life. After I left the record company I discovered that my cousin was selling T-shirt heat-sealed transfers. He explained that he's buying them for fifteen cents and selling them for seventy-five cents. It seemed like a nice margin. He said to me, 'I will sell them to you for twenty cents. I'll make a nickel on you and you can make a buck.'"

"I took some of my savings and bought transfers. I went into a store on Young Street in Toronto that sold T-shirts. That's how the T-shirt business started for me. Then I called my friend, who owned this record store in Montreal. I talked to him about what I was doing and he and I went into business together. We would run around and sell transfers and had a nice little business going. For a young guy, it was a very good business, but our partnership was always volatile and as a result it really did not work, and after a couple of years we broke it up."

Second Business—"My own little agency"

Selling heat transfers for T-shirts eventually evolved into the clothing agency (wholesale) business. Joel's career is marked by a pattern of social connections with people who become business relationships and partners.

"It was around this time that I bumped into Gary Hurwitz. He and I became good friends. He owned a major clothing company, based in Toronto. I knew nothing about clothing—and I still don't—but he took me in and I did extremely well working there. I earned a lot of money selling that stuff. Then I met other sales guys who had multiple clothing lines. I learned that you can get multiple lines if you have an agency. So I opened up my own little agency. My first year was terrible because I didn't know the business. Then I had one line that was really hot, Sergio Valente. I also had one line I carried that went bankrupt owing me a lot of money. And then other guys didn't pay me. I learned that you have to pay your dues on the road. I guess I paid my dues in my first year. I lost $15,000."

Joel is the master of bouncing back. "I lost lots of money and was forced to sell some of my coveted record collection to cover my debts." This setback did not slow him down. Joel used the situation as a learning opportunity and used the knowledge to open and run his next agency.

"A colleague of mine was making Flashdance clothing [based on the 1983 movie]. The clothing became a symbol to the young people. It was a whole new fashion thing. Everybody wanted to emulate the movie. If you remember, it was all that off-the-shoulder clothes, and striped shorts, and tights. Anyway, I went to see him because I needed more work. He gave me a territory in Southwestern Ontario."

Joel was careful to ensure that he was putting the building blocks together. "There was this guy, Norman Kamen, who took me under his wing. He, too, is my friend to this day. Norman was known as the 'father of the road,' and with his help I became the de facto, 'son of the road.' There was also Jack Heaton and he was known as the 'grandfather of the road.' These guys liked me and if you worked with Norman or Jack you became successful because you were associated with them."

Business Three: Things Really Take Off—Backstage Pass

"I was having fun, but I was also thinking about doing something different. I had a plan, not really a plan, more like a dream. Around this time, I became friends with a guy named Brent. He was the father of one of my son's best friends. Brent was a really nice guy, so I felt comfortable telling him this idea I had. Brent thought it was brilliant, and asked if he could be involved. Well, to me this was all an exercise in futility because it was just not going to happen, but somehow it did."

"For my new vision to become a reality several unlikely events had to take place. Our plan was to open up a store called "Backstage Pass" that would do rock and roll merchandising. This was new and innovative. Nobody in Canada was doing this. Brent and I developed a concept and a business plan, but we needed financing. I was able to enlist the help of my friend Neil who owned a record label. Today Neil runs Canada Music Week and is still prominent in the music scene. Neil introduced Brent and me to Bill Graham, of Fillmore East fame and Del Furano, who would later work for Sony Records. We were getting excited as we felt like we were talking to the right people."

"To structure the deal, Del said, 'You guarantee me $50,000 of royalty money, and you take my roster.' This was the start we needed. Del's roster had about 500 rock and roll bands on it. His roster included the Beatles, the Rolling Stones, Led Zeppelin, etc."

"We had no money because we had mortgaged our homes to get started, and that's all we had. So we tried to sell half the business to get funding for it, which we did. The investors, our partners, put up half the money. So we sold off 50 percent of the business. We had to make it work. Backstage Pass opened up in 1987. We were successful out of the gate. The first year we did two million. The second year we did twelve million. We were selling to the major retailers. Year number two, we were blessed with the New Kids on the Block. They were phenomenal. It was like the Beatles. It was New Kids mania. We used to travel with them, and it was like living in the eye of a hurricane. I mean, I finally understood what it meant to be a Beatle, living with these guys was an insane life, but it was great."

"We were also selling at shows. Now we were doing both. We were merchandising through retailers and selling at shows. We were growing, hiring staff, and traveling everywhere. We were getting our act together. Our run lasted 11 years. It was mostly wonderful. And I will never forget it."

"Here's a lesson about the economics of selling at a rock and roll venue. When you sell goods there, typically the venue takes between 40 and 50 percent of the selling price. That's forty dollars per shirt today, so approximately twenty bucks goes to the venue. Now if it's a superstar like Bruce Springsteen, for example, because of his name, he wants 45 percent royalty. But he'll take the 45 percent royalty off of the forty dollar price. This is how this whole thing works. So now you've got forty-five points off of forty. That leaves eighteen bucks. And you have twenty bucks that the venue is taking, and there is two bucks and change left for you. You have to make the shirt and get the shirt there so there's not a big margin. And if there are leftovers, you lose. Fortunately, most bands take a 20 percent deal. For every shirt we sell for superstars you might lose thirty-one cents per shirt. But then we have that star on our roster. Then you go to the next band and you say, we want you on our roster and they ask 'Who's with you? Bruce Springsteen. Oh, okay.' They know you are legitimate when you have that cycle working for you. You keep moving and adding to the cycle."

"We were successful, but in the first year or two there were struggles. We were zooming along by the seat of our pants. Then we got our own building and that helped. We had a sauna and a whirlpool in the office. Remember, we were a rock and roll company! Backstage Pass represented over 500 bands and we did all the merchandising. Not only did we take care of their retail items, but we would also go on tour with the groups. I hired the staff that would travel with the bands. We were the guys selling you those extremely high-priced T-shirts, overpriced hats, and stuff."

The End of a Great Run

"We had a great run, especially in this kind of business, but eventually, after eleven years, things fell apart. It was really a combination of many things. My partner Brent started having serious personal problems. One day this highly intelligent and successful entrepreneur who wore a business suit everyday started showing up for work looking like John Lennon, glasses and all. It was a transformation of his personality. It was freaking me and everyone else out. We were disagreeing about everything. It got so bad between us that we actually drew a line down our office floor separating both sides. To make matters worse, we found out we were being embezzled by our financial officer. Everything was out of control. We had grown so big so fast. At this time we were at about $25 million and we were losing control of managing the operation. With all the chaos Brent and I were not even speaking to each other. I could not go on the way it was. Our agreement with Del and Bill was that we went to their company, Winterland, in San Francisco every three or four months to review the state of the business. At what would turn out to be our last regular visit to them, I walked in and Michael Krasner, who was their head of legal, looked up at us and things were so bad that it was obvious from the look on his face that there was something very wrong. That was the moment we knew it was over."

"With excellent professional help, we were able to dissolve the business without much of a hassle. Funny thing is despite all this, Michael Krasner became business partners with me in my new company and is one of my best friends, even after all these years later. Brent and I didn't stay in touch, but there was a nice article about him in the paper recently. I'm pleased about that."

Close a Door and Open Another

"In closing Backstage Pass, one of the people I needed to contact was a colleague named Steve Kumar. Steve was our key distributor to the independent market. We could not deal with the independent retail stores in Canada. We could sell to The Bay and Sears and Wal-Mart and those guys, but the independents were a different world. Steve was my exclusive distributor to them."

Joel's plan for the meeting with Steve was to tell him about the end of "Backstage Pass" and to make Steve a very generous offer. "I was going to give Steve all the Canadian rights that I had—for free. I explained to him, 'It's yours. We have been friends for a long time and I am not going to charge you for any of it because I don't work that way.' I told him that if he needs any help, I would be a phone call away, and I would guide him through it."

Business Four: The House—Friends Make Business Partners

"To my surprise Steve said, 'I am a multi-millionaire and I really love working with you. You have been my friend as well, and for you to even do this for me is unbelievable. Why don't I put up all the money, you put up your knowledge, and we will do this a second time, only with me and you as partners.' Right there at the table we shook hands and to this day we have a handshake deal. It was 'The House' rising out of the ashes of 'Backstage Pass.' 'Backstage Pass' closed on January 27, 1997. 'The House' opened up four days later."

"It was amazing. I was meeting with Steve to tell him good-bye. I was saying I will be moving to California, and then a few magic words from Steve and I am right back in it."

"'The House' is a licensed apparel company. We own the Canadian apparel rights for a number of comic book, movie, and TV properties. Of course we still work with my old standard rock and roll bands. We own the Canadian rights for the Beatles. For example, if you want to buy a Beatles T-shirt and it's a legitimate licensed Beatle T-shirt in Canada, they come from my company. Same thing is true with a Batman or Superman kid shirt and with "The Family Guy" and "The Simpsons." It all evolved nicely out of 'Backstage Pass.'"

The CEO

Joel's education, his charm, his gift with people, and his ability to survive multiple business setbacks all evolved out of a childhood shaped by his parent's horrific ordeals during World War II.

In Joel's case, his parents experiences and values shaped his future. "My dad, Nathan, came to America from Poland after the war. He could not speak a word of English. He worked as a peddler and would go door-to-door selling. He sold notions and lotions and potions, as well as apparel. He learned English as he was earning a living. He would talk in Polish, and he would point to certain things he was showing to his customers and they would tell him, 'No, this is the English word.' Somehow during this time he found his way to Montreal, Canada. He met and married my mother, who was Canadian, but she was born of Russian parents, who had escaped the Czars. So she had an Eastern European background as well. Maybe because of the oppression they faced growing up, my parents gave me a lot of freedom throughout my childhood."

Joel learned how to survive at home from his parents. "My dad was a survivor of the Holocaust. He was in Auschwitz and had his prisoner number tattooed on his arm by the Nazis. He came from a family of 14 children; 13 perished in the ovens. At one point my father and grand-father were being loaded on to a train to the death camps. My grand-father knew this was the end for him, so before he went on the train, my grandfather gave my father a ring with initials on it. He wanted my dad to have it for a keepsake. Then, to save his life, my grandfather pushed my father underneath the train so he would be out of sight. My father survived on leaves and berries for many months, but he was finally captured. While on the run his weight dropped to 65 pounds. He was emaciated and his fingers were all deformed. When my father was captured by the Nazis they said to him, take off your ring. Because his fingers were all puffy, he couldn't, so the Nazis chopped his finger off and threw the ring back at him. So he's missing a finger, and he still has the tattoo. There are many, many horror stories he did not share with me until recently. Today he's 87 and it has taken him all these many years to talk about it. Interesting thing, I never heard him complain."

Like Father Like Son

"My father opened a store in 1960. He had a business partner. They were never great friends. They were just good partners, but they were never pals. Well, I have a partner now, and it is the exact same thing. We are good partners but we are not best friends. My Dad's business was a convenience store called the Pastry and Delicatessen Shop. It was an upscale convenience store that sold fresh pastries, breads, bagels, cold cuts, as well as milk, eggs, butter and soft drinks. He ran it for 30 years."

"My uncle was the closest person to me in my childhood. He was even closer to me than my father and mother. My uncle lived in my house. I had a weird childhood growing up. My grandmother, my uncle, my mother, my father, and my sister, and I all lived in a pretty small house. My uncle and I shared the same bedroom, but he was never around because he owned a modeling agency, and he was always out with the models."

"My uncle was my mother's brother. He, too, was an entrepreneur and was a big influence on me. He, like Ringo, was my hero. My uncle was great. He saw that I did not have a father who was ever around, or who I could do anything with, because he was always working, and he filled the void and became my surrogate dad. When the movie *A Hard Day's Night* came out, he took me to see it. I made him sit through it three times, which he did without complaint."

"Being in the modeling business he knew many famous people. He was friends with the coach of the Montreal Canadiens hockey team and he would take me to their practices. Being a kid, they would give me hockey sticks and pucks and all kinds of things. I used this stuff unaware that they would be my first collectables or that these could have been worth thousands of dollars. Years later, I ran into one of these stars and I said, 'When I was seven years old, you gave me your hockey stick, and I want you to know what a wonderful gesture it was, and I just want to say thank you.' The guy, said, 'I don't recall doing that,' and walked away. Here I was, opening my heart to the guy, saying, you were my hero, and he tells me to take a hike. I would have to say that that experience had a big effect on me. Maybe it also served to reinforce that music was my great interest in life."

"My business advisor and best friend always tells me that one of the things that makes me unique is that I built my career on who I am and did not compromise or change my personality. Music changed everything for me. I collected thousands of records. It was the whole British 60s thing, Peter and Gordon, the Yardbirds, the Mindbenders, Chad and Jeremy, the Dave Clark Five, Jerry and the Pacemakers, and, of course, the Beatles. They became the sound track of my life. Some songs obviously had a little bit more meaning than others for me. I would really listen to those, and they helped shape me as a person. My formal education was in religious schools, which I had no use for. My real education occurred through the music I listened to. I know I am not the only one that was affected by this phenomenon. There is a great book about this called *Growing up with the Beatles* by Ron Schaumburg.It's all about that."

"My name is in *The Beatles Anthology*. These wonderful guys asked me to help them with the merchandise for *Anthology 1*. It was a great opportunity and I got to meet Neil Aspinall, who was regarded as the fifth Beatle. Neil was their road manager in 1961 and stayed with them through the years at Apple Records. And there was Mike Heatley, who was a guy from EMI Records [part of the world's largest independent music company]. He was really the person in charge of the Beatles music catalog. Mike was the guy who connected me to the Beatles. I didn't have anything to do professionally with Ringo or the Beatles, but he knew what it would mean to me to meet Ringo, and one day he called me and said, 'Hey, I want to get you backstage. I want you to meet Ringo.'"

"It was nice. Everyone has heroes. For me it was the Beatles. They have been for most of my life. And when I got to meet Ringo, I just stood there and I gushed. I looked at him and said you're my hero, and I love you, and I am in the music business. Here is the unbelievable part. He just said, 'You know, I'm huggable,' and I gave him a huge, big hug, and I wasn't letting go. My wife says that the security guards had to separate us. I want to tell you, right after that moment, I walked away and started crying. I just broke down in tears. Because it was nice to see that the guy I had put my love and faith in for all those years turned out to be a really sweet guy, the guy who I hoped he would be."

"My record collection is amazing. This is really my second record collection. I had sold off a lot of my first collection when I was broke, but I never sold the Beatles. My current Beatles collection is in a twenty-foot by twenty-foot room and it is filled ceiling to floor. There are pictures of me and Paul, shots with me and Ringo, letters to me from George Harrison, correspondence from John Lennon, gold albums and platinum records."

Message and Lessons

Deals Based on Trust

"I have made most of my deals with a handshake. All the deals I have with Fox and Warner Brothers are all handshakes. I am one of the only people in my industry who works like that. A record industry executive and I were in L.A. trying to do a deal. We could never do it. I thought his terms were just outlandish, so I called him up and said, 'Let's have lunch.' He said, 'Rabinowitz, I want to eat with you. I don't want to have a deal with you.' I told him that that was fine, but I still like you as a guy so let's go for lunch and have fun. After the lunch, he said, 'Come to my office now and we will work on your terms.' At his office I pull out a napkin from lunch, and it said, 'Joel paid 16 percent and he will get

$100,000 a year, and this will go on in perpetuity. That was our deal. This was a multi-billion dollar firm. We're writing napkin deals. That's how I like to work."

Joel believes it is important to stay focused on your goals. "I think it goes back to karma. What goes around comes around. I try to treat everybody I meet with respect. That's my religion. Treat people the way you want to be treated. Now I am well over twelve years into my partnership with Steve Kumar, and we have not had a formal agreement. We still only have a handshake."

For Joel, things were constantly changing, and he learned early that you need to adapt your plan. "There's still a lot to do with this business, but it's a recessionary time now. The model for how we need to work is changing daily. Retailers are changing daily. Retailers seem to be blaming the suppliers if goods are not selling. And in this economy it's all getting more and more goofy. To keep me sane and looking at the future I have gotten together with two other guys and we're working on a merchandising deal related to a big movie that will be coming out in the summer, and a new garment product that is going to revolutionize the sports apparel industry."

Summary

There are a few things that are completely obvious from being with Joel and his story. He is a totally charming and entertaining human being who makes people around him laugh like a child and feel energized and special. He effortlessly turns casual acquaintances into business friends, business relationships, and partners over and over again. People want to work with him because he's fun to be around, has a vision, business strategy, connections, energy, and integrity.

Joel had a mission in life: to enjoy life and be around music. But there is a raging fire that burns within him to always be accomplishing something. He is committed to living his passions in a big way. His parents taught him how to survive hardship and to Joel, being an entrepreneur means that failure is never an option and that makes entrepreneurship less risky. He is driven more by intuitive instincts combined with years of experience. Joel is more than business plans, but when he needed a business plan, he has produced excellent ones. He has run incredibly complicated businesses, created new niche markets, and taken good care of his friends and family all with a flair and ease that might confuse others into thinking that he got lucky. Even Joel is quick to attribute his success to 'being in the right place at the right time.' He is as shrewd, driven, obsessed, calculating, and ethical as the most steely-eyed business mogul you can imagine, but because of his childish charm you rarely see that side of him. There is a special place in the 24-Hour entrepreneurs' hall of fame for the person who lives his dreams, breaks through barriers, turns dreams into reality, invites you along for the ride, and sounds like he's having nothing but fun doing it.

Authors's 24-Hour Turnaround Score: 85

Joel's Leadership Principles:

- ∞ Parents provide a values base for the future and they teach the skills to survive

- ∞ Never give up

- ∞ Stay focused on your goals

- ∞ Stay focused on the future

- ∞ Treat people fairly and the way you want to be treated

- ∞ Let the horse run free—don't put boundaries round your dreams

- ∞ It boils down to economics—know the margins and stay a step ahead of everyone else

- ∞ Work from your strengths, live your dreams and have fun

- ∞ Stay true to your personality. Never stop being a child

- ∞ If one door closes, don't worry as another one opens

Image 11: Joel and Ringo 1989

Chapter 6: From Star Struck to Entrepreneurial Star

Image 12: Paul and Joel

Chapter 6: From Star Struck to Entrepreneurial Star

7 Using a Higher Purpose to Create Greatness

Russell Robinson, CEO, Jewish National Fund (JNF), (http://www.jnf.org)

The Jewish National Fund

Jewish National Fund is a nonprofit organization founded in 1901. It all started with the actions of Theodor Herzl, a Viennese journalist. Herzl witnessed a series of well-publicized and particularly virulent anti-Semitic acts happening across Europe. He believed it was time to take action and was determined that a fund needed to be established to purchase land for a Jewish State in Ottoman-controlled Palestine.

Over the past 109 years, the JNF has evolved into a global environmental leader by planting 240 million trees, building over 240 reservoirs and dams, developing over 250,000 acres of land, creating more than 1,000 parks, and providing the infrastructure for over 1,000 communities. Another part of its mission is educating people around the world about Israel and the environment.

The CEO

David is happy to face Goliath. All business leaders are driven to achieve something. Russell Robinson was driven to rescue an organization he held precious even though it was in crisis. This job was not his only option, but for Russell there was a special calling to work with the Jewish National Fund. The JNF's organizational history had made it most widely known for "Blue Boxes" (local fundraising collections) and the "Tree Drive," the "Plant a tree in Israel" fundraising campaign. He knew at the outset that this was not going to be just another job. He knew that as CEO he was signing up for the adventure of a lifetime that would require and demand all he had to give. What he didn't know completely was how deeply troubled the organization he inherited was.

"Early on, my CFO (who had come here only a month and a half before I did) and I were here until three o'clock in the morning trying to figure out what bills to pay. So for the first six months, I had no plan. The only phone calls we were getting were from bill collectors. We had a big wall full of yellow stickies and we'd list all the people we owed. One day he came to my office and said, 'Do you want the good news or the bad news?' I said, 'Well, what's the bad news?' He said, 'We only have $225 in the bank, but the good news is we still have a few weeks until payroll.' I'm proud to say that today we have no debt."

The organization was clearly in terrible shape, but as it turned out, Russell was exactly the right kind of leader to take on this job.

"My father taught me a couple of things. First off, he taught me to never sell anybody anything. Always help them buy. My father sold stereos and he built his business by understanding that it's a matter of what they want to buy, not what you're selling them. He also taught me, your competition is only yourself. Chase your competition and you'll chase yourself out of business."

"I grew up on the other side of the tracks, in a small town in Texas called El Paso with a Jewish community of 1,300 [people]. My parents didn't have much and I think that that builds you into what you will become. You have to struggle, you have to fight, you have to know that there are goals, and that you're going to have to make it on your own. As part of a small, misunderstood minority, I came to realize that I hated my Judaism for reasons that made a lot of sense to me as a kid. One way of trying to fit in was to play sports. I played football and baseball but it's tough when the thing that gets in your way is your Judaism. The problem was that I had to go to religious study class in the afternoon. I'm playing for a football coach who was meeting the only Jew that he has ever met, and I'm telling him that I can't come on Wednesday for practice because I'm going to Judaism class, which sounds to him like something from Mars. Because of this degree of unfamiliarity, I found myself educating others about Judaism. So there was nothing positive about being a Jew back then. In some ways this accounted for my independence."

This desire to be independent was a guiding principle and would later shape Russell's leadership style. "I completely funded my own college education. And that's when I started my own business. I started a carpet cleaning business out of necessity. I needed money."

From an early age Russell had the instincts of an entrepreneur. "Our small carpet cleaning business took over all the other, much bigger companies. We were beating them because we didn't worry about the competition. We focused on being the best. You have to believe in what you're delivering and then deliver it as best you can. Eventually I was running several different businesses. I didn't really have the training to do any of it."

"As far as the rest of the family, my mother worked all her life. She worked as a store manager. My brothers are entrepreneurs like me. So I think it's in the family, in the genes, and the thought process. I got into fundraising because of a guy from the United Jewish Appeal (UJA). At the time, I was running a UJA fundraising campaign. I was responsible for the community campaign, just as a volunteer professional. It wasn't my job, but I liked it. Somehow it fit into my vision of wanting to become a great leader and change the world." Through Russell's drive, initiative and business skills, he progressed rapidly up the ranks of the UJA. "I was hired as a director in the Southern region, then I took over the West, and then became the national fundraising director."

Company History

The JNF has gone through many transitions through its long history. When Russell became CEO in 1997, the organization was severely outdated. "I think that about seven months into my time with the organization my CFO and I sat in a room. I thought he was going to quit. Every time we tried to fix a problem, something else bad would happen. But I encouraged him, he helped me, and we got through it."

"There was no effective organizational structure, no reliable record-keeping, little computerization, and a host of people who were totally unprepared for what it meant to run and work in a successful nonprofit. I knew going in that I had to make changes, both organizationally and with regard to key roles, but so much was broken that I had to be clear with my plan on where to start."

"There were people who had given their life and been with our organization for thirty or forty years. Whatever problems we had were not their fault. They worked as hard as they could and did what they were asked to do. So the toughest thing I had to do early on was to make the decision that I had to let people go. I didn't believe we could survive with the staff we had, but the faces of the people I had to let go are still in my thoughts. They'll always be with me. So I tell people all the time, if you don't take hiring very seriously, you'll regret it. It should be as serious as firing. The first year we eliminated well over 200 positions on the staff. It was a necessary business decision. I made the judgment that anybody who had worked with JNF for over thirty years, which was a lot of them, I would do the firing myself. I flew around the country, I had to dismiss people, I was closing offices, it was very difficult, and I was brand new into it. But I needed to be the one to do it."

Russell wanted to send a clear message. "The remaining staff needed to see that the actions I was taking were about saving the whole organization and ultimately, the jobs of everyone else. I also needed to demonstrate that we were transitioning to a new culture of action and decisive leadership. When I joined we had 350 employees. Today we have a total of 161, including our maintenance staff and security guards. It was a painful time, but it was necessary. When I joined JNF, we were failing. Today we are a top-ranked nonprofit. We have the American Philanthropy A+ rating."

Problems and Challenges

"To ensure the survival of the JNF, the first thing I needed to do was get its finances in order. Ronald Lauder [former JNF president, philanthropist and CEO of Estée Lauder] made substantial gifts to us at first, because we couldn't even borrow money. That gave us the first six months. Even then, though I was pretty new in the CEO role, I knew where we were headed. Today we are still on the same course."

"I had a plan for getting out of debt, and going from an organization in distress to a well-run, highly functioning business, we needed to fix things based on priority. Today we have a financial plan. We always have a five-year rolling plan, so we know where our expenses are. You can always calculate your expenses out for five years and that way there are fewer surprises. You know that if you're spending one hundred dollars there's going to be a 5 percent increase on insurance, rent, paper and so on, so you're at $105. If you don't raise $105 you're out of business. I'm a numbers person. I always have been, I always know what my goals are because I have to. There's a certain number that you have to bring in. Every day the cash receipts come to me and I communicate them. I believe in sharing the data and sending it out. I believe in the 'print, circle, and comment' approach to management. That means that in my regular communication to the staff, I circle the critical information and say, this is what we did, this is what we need to do. What do you think?"

"This organization is more than just about money. It can't just be about balancing the books. To accomplish the JNF mission we needed to build a strong infrastructure that would move us successfully toward the next hundred years. Now my greatest challenge is change, and this is true for all nonprofits. It's not just raising money for poor children. That's important to us, but the bigger goal for the long-term survival of the organization is about the partnerships with our donors. This means that for the JNF to succeed it has to have an image and presence that's appealing to multiple generations and age groups."

"Technology plays a tremendous role in being successful. When I started we were in the technology dark ages. We had to not only catch up, but find a way to stay at the front. It's something that's very hard to get your hands around. Our web services are now among the best in our industry. We're always trying to stay ahead, but it's not easy to figure out what is and what isn't important. Yesterday we had a marketing meeting to discuss this. I also have roundtables with other nonprofits to compare notes. I think that we can touch people. We can touch somebody from their birth to their passing. I feel that our organization is ready to have that kind of connectivity."

"You don't have to have all the money in the world to make an impact. But you have to use the money well. So we learned to work with the government in Israel to have them match our contributions. That's one example of a critical partnership. And sometimes we're the catalyst. You don't have to be the only one working for a solution. As a matter of fact, it doesn't normally happen that way. You don't have to wait for a government to make it happen. In the United States we don't, nor in Israel. Democracies need nonprofits to be catalysts for change. Goodwill Industries, for example, services the poor better than the government services the unfortunate. It's just a reality. Governments are not good at everything."

Strategic and Action Steps

Planning had four main dimensions for Russell. First, a strategic plan that reflected the consensus of the organization; second, a vision that people could relate to; third, an approach to increasing inclusion, build commitment, and facilitate more effective communication; and last, a top-management team that he could work with and a revamped board of directors.

1. **Strategic Planning:** "We've already had two and we're now talking about the third long-term strategic planning process in an eleven-year period. Part of the strategy is not just trying to change the direction of the organization, but we're trying to bring people along to where the organization is."

   "It is never easy stepping back and doing strategic planning. This tough economy isn't the best time to think strategically. But sometimes it's good to do planning when there are big questions. I also like to have these meetings when we're doing very well, which ironically, is also a time when people don't want to plan. They question, 'Why do this now when things are good?' Well, that's the time to do it. That's when you're thinking openly and you can really have people express themselves freely."

   "There are several objectives we need to accomplish for strategic meetings. First is obviously updating the current plan. These meetings are also an opportunity to bring our diverse management group together, to have challenging discussions about what our new challenges may be, how they will continue to learn and grow professionally, and how best to accomplish our mission."

2. **Establish a vision:** "I don't think that our vision has changed all that much. It's now stated more clearly, but it's still the same message. Even in the midst of all the turmoil. I was fascinated to find out that this organization drew all these people, had all this support, for trees and blue boxes. That very compelling approach drew them in. Even though our press was awful, we stuck with our strategic plan and stayed focused. We were still raising money and we still had a lot of people involved. Our product was fairly simple in the sense that, in the broadest terms, it was the land and people of Israel."

3. **Establish a more effective board of directors:** "In the past, of course, we had a board of directors. At the time it was 390 members. No 390-person board is going to be able to make decisions. We now have a much smaller board of directors, which has allowed us to become the professional business we are today. They meet monthly to advise, set policy, express their opinions and ask tough questions. They empower me to lead and make decisions. I hire. I fire. I'm responsible for everything we do. If it's not working, I'm the one to blame."

4. **Inclusion:** "I was aware that greater inclusion was an important goal. We needed to get groups like the lay leaders more involved in direction-setting. This resulted in a series of big, ongoing, comprehensive strategy meetings. When I introduced these meetings I knew it would be challenging to get a growing circle of people energetic and committed to communicating the goals of the JNF. We have 1,400 active lay leaders. The meetings have been starting to work. For almost a year and a half we've been consistently sending out updates about what we accomplished and where we are headed. Now we're into it. It's interesting because we saw that we've fulfilled about 90 percent of the things that people have said we should focus on. We also have a legal group. It's twenty-two lawyers who get together every month on the phone, or in person, and deal with all of our legal issues. That is an example of inclusion."

"Running an organization like the JNF means having a broad world view. We're almost at 600,000 donors. Everywhere I go in the United States, I talk about the future of the Jewish community. I see that so many people want to be connected. The work goes well beyond the Jewish community. We've had the Pope visit Israel and did a mass with people of the Nazareth. The rabbis are involved and the Muslims as well. We're redoing Abraham's well, which is important to Islam, Judaism, and Christianity. One little place, Israel. There's no land anywhere like that in the world."

Taking Risks

"In my early nonprofit years, one of my jobs was visiting with refuseniks in the former Soviet Union [Jews who were protesting the treatment of Jews in the Soviet Union]. We used to bring merchandise to them. Merchandise was brand new blue jeans. A brand new pair of blue jeans would get a refusenik enough money on the black market for them to live on for one or two months. This was necessary because they weren't allowed to work."

"Almost 400,000 Romanians moved to Israel between 1948 and the fall of former Romanian President Nicolae Ceausescu, who said that Jews were a better business than cattle because he got paid more for the Jews. The real unbelievable story was how to bring 400,000 people out of a communist country. Ceausescu was a business person, so his government worked out the deal. It was very risky business."

"It was around this time that I learned of Ronald Lauder. He was doing work in Eastern Europe and I met him one time in Poland. Jews from the Soviet Union and other places were going there. If Ronald didn't do his work in Budapest, Poland, and other places, you would have had just a very weak community. Today you have strength in the communities that are there."

"I didn't meet Ronald Lauder until I was leaving the United Jewish Appeal. Coincidently I got a phone call from him asking me to come for twenty minutes to talk about the selection of a new CEO for the Jewish National Fund. When I got to his office he spent three hours telling me I should be starting on Monday as the new CEO for the JNF. I tried telling him that I didn't even know what job he was talking about. Ronald never takes 'no' easily, so later on that day he called me to come into the office. He said there were eighteen people from the search committee on the phone. The next thing I knew I was having an interview with the search committee on the telephone for a job I didn't even know I was interviewing for. He asked me to show up in two days for a meeting. I thought it was going to be a meeting with three people.

It turned out to be another twenty people. He kept telling me when I was starting. I kept telling him I had another job offer for another organization and I didn't want to move permanently to New York. He kept telling me my start date. Lo and behold, he won."

Russell knew he had the strong support of the JNF leadership, but in the beginning, his role was to re-build the organization and set the direction for future success. "I knew that everything was on the table at this point and could fall apart. Whatever goodwill I had developed could easily have been wiped away due to poor implementation."

"When I started, we had offices and no database. Some people had data terminals on their desk, but we only owned two PCs. This was 1998. They were so far behind in adapting to technology. There was a memo in the personnel manual that said that if you were found with a PC or a laptop, you'd be fired. Good people were making very bad business decisions. I think this is common in nonprofits. They had hired people who were in the social work and social service business. I had to get people to understand the connections between the cause, the people, and good business practices. What they were missing was an understanding of the dollar and cents of what we were doing. We were in terrible debt. We did not have a strong central organization. Every city had a different logo. Every office was quoting different prices for trees. [At the time, the sale of trees for Israel was a main income source for the JNF.] They all handled the tree sales independently."

"First I had them calculate how long it takes to obtain a tree order, how long and what kind of order was it. It was taking twenty-three minutes for an order. Trees were then probably about 25 percent of our income. It's today less than 5 percent. We discovered that there were still hundreds of thousands of people ordering trees. And we weren't even advertising that well. The good news was that everybody knew the JNF. The bad news, everybody knew us for trees and blue boxes. The worst news was that we were losing $4.90 every time we sold a tree. And we were doing it in great volume! So we raised the price of trees. With that as a start we began to get a handle on costs and income."

Leadership Style

Russell recognized that to be a catalyst for change, it was necessary for him to lead by example. He knew, from the beginning, that lack of accountability among the staff was an issue. "I was determined to demonstrate to the organization that I would hold them accountable for their actions. More importantly, I wanted them to see that I was holding myself to those same, if not higher, standards." He emphasized this as a key principle.

"One of the hardest things I had to do was the decision that I would deliver layoff notices to long-tenured employees in person. It was an unpleasant job, but it demonstrated my leadership and compassion and that I would not delegate difficult tasks." Another key 24-Hour Principle that Russell introduced to the organization was the concept of openness and sharing. He wanted to convince people that it was inevitable that he and everyone else would make mistakes, sometimes big mistakes, but if they could be open and honest with each other about it, they would all learn from each other and ultimately make the JNF stronger.

"I taught them that my belief is that if you didn't make mistakes, you hadn't tried anything." This concept represented a big cultural shift, so it was a very important and symbolic part of Russell's plan to transform the organization. His push for accountability and to be a top-notch business organization also related to his fundamental goals. There were many parts in motion: re-building the organization, hiring the right staff, and spending time with the community. But for Russell, his foremost goal was staying focused on why the JNF existed and his role in carrying that torch.

"I always tell people, you have to look at everything that you're doing as if it were your own business. So I try to get the staff to think in those terms."

From the start Russell knew where the JNF should be headed, but he was equally concerned about how they got there. He was convinced that above everything else, because of their mission, the management of the JNF had to be values-based. As an organization they had to know what they stood for.

"You have to have integrity. Our purpose is to take somebody's philanthropic dollars. That means that we're having a discussion with somebody on a very intimate level. We're talking to them about money, their inner feelings, their desires, dreams, hopes, and what they want to accomplish regarding their relationship with the JNF. That's a tremendous responsibility and that's where integrity has to fit."

In re-building the JNF, Russell took on the role of mentor as well as leader. He worked tirelessly to inspire as many people as he could to make a commitment to the organization. Like the other 24-Hour leaders, there was an issue of personal and professional balance. Russell made many personal sacrifices.

For Russell that means asking whether he has also served his family and himself. "There was a story once written about being between two loves. When you love your job and you love your family, you're between two loves. I think that there are always those family issues with any job. You have to believe what you're doing. You have to believe in who you are and in your family. I'm doing the family piece. I don't know if I have done it 100 percent right or wrong. I've had my talks with my kids about all of this. You try to be everywhere. I remember when I used to travel all the time. One year I was living in L.A. and New York, so I used to fly back to L.A. on weekends and watch the kids' baseball and softball games. I might [have been] sleepy, but they knew I was there and how much effort it took to get there."

Message and Lessons

Russell's work with the JNF started with an organization fighting to pay the bills; as it grew more successful, he then had to deal with building new systems and re-bolstering the infrastructure. "In an organization like ours, the work is never done because what needs to be accomplished is never finished—there are always more projects." There are projects to initiate and manage, donors to talk to, meetings, dinners, speeches, and a nonstop series of events and visits, all designed to clarify and deliver the mission and the message.

"Today, there certainly are more projects than ever before, but it's different now because there is a lot more at stake, expectations are higher, and everything we do has increased complexity. The crises are more external and we are geared up to respond." With this success also comes the opportunity to reflect on redefining the strategy and projects as well as values. He joined the JNF when it was at a crossroads and on the brink of failure. Today it is a top-rated charity by the independent nonprofit rating service "Charity Navigator." "When an organization is involved with a tough economy like we have today, it does not mean we can slow down our projects and turn our backs on the commitments we made. The donations still need to come in. It means reminding people of our bigger mission, and that to accomplish our good deeds we need money."

Summary

When Russell joined the JNF, commitment met opportunity at the bottom of a huge mountain. He has worked step-by-step to move the organization to the top of the nonprofit world. Russell is fearless in mission and has shown that he is not inclined to give up in the face of doubt and overwhelming odds. In fact, one of the fastest ways to get his attention is to tell him that something cannot be done. That quality alone demonstrates why he has been so successful.

He learned about good business practices and customer satisfaction by watching his father run a stereo business. He started his own business at a young age and taught himself the essentials of being an entrepreneur by assuming the leadership role and learning-by-doing. His good-natured, magnetic charm seems to have come naturally. Part of the reason that, from the beginning, Russell fit so perfectly with the JNF's mission was because he understood five critical things:

1. The organization's debt and the weight of its financial problems. The only way to fix things was by careful prioritization. Before he could begin working his way through the long list of crises, Russell realized that getting finances in order was top priority.
2. How to plan and strategize. Russell set a new plan and strategy that would be implemented with metrics and accountability.
3. A smaller, tighter-knit organization would work more efficiently than a large one. Russell understood that he needed to make significant personnel changes.

4. To build a more inclusive and committed group, he needed to open up the staff's communication system and welcome feedback.

5. Technology would play a key role in moving the organization forward.

The reassuring part about Russell is that no matter what crisis the JNF may face, it is clear that he is up to the challenge. He will be there to utilize the resources necessary to accomplish the task at hand, communicate with clarity, and recognize the team around him. All this goes on while he accepts the heavy personal burden that having a higher sense of social responsibility takes. It means knowing that whatever you are working on is about to be interrupted by another urgent phone call that cannot possibly wait, because whatever it is, it must be really important.

Author's 24-Hour Turnaround Score: 95

Russell Robinson's 24-Hour Leadership Principles:

∞ Leadership skills develop early in life

∞ Core values come from within

∞ Tackle the mess—fix things sequentially, but play to your strengths

∞ Watch the financials like a hawk

∞ Hire people carefully and create a culture of openness and sharing

∞ Build on a solid vision and never stop believing

∞ Be a catalyst for change

∞ Everyone has to be working toward the same goals

∞ Balance your work and your personal life

∞ Leaders make tough decisions

∞ Lead by example; do as I say and as I do

Image 13: Russell with Prime Minister Ehud Olmert

Image 14: Russell with Prime Minister Yitzhak Shamir

Image 15: Russell with Ronald Lauder

Image 16: Russell with Prime Minister Ariel Sharon

Chapter 7: Using a Higher Purpose to Create Greatness

8 The Road to Success in 24 Hours

The premise of the leadership stories in this book is that when you honestly embrace change and the achievement of entrepreneurial success, you can see the beginnings of organizational improvement in as little as 24 hours.

The spirit of entrepreneurs, these people we call economic heroes, and the foundation of our economy are all about growing, changing, and continuously improving. The stories in the previous chapters were about highly successful entrepreneurs. They all had setbacks, some even suffered crushing failures. They all struggled to overcome big obstacles, but persevered. In some cases, the hurdles they needed to overcome were an outdated business plan, a family member, a messy move, the wrong team, a lack of vision on the part of a predecessor, or just bad timing. These leaders led decisively and learned from prior mistakes. They trusted the plan and their instincts to do the right thing and they understood what Nelson Mandela meant when he said, *"The greatest glory in living lies not in never falling, but in rising every time we fall."*

These are leaders who saw themselves as part of the solution, with little regard for the odds. As true entrepreneurs they paid a big price for their success. They have had to trade business for family more times than they would wish. They all have struggled with the loneliness of leadership. Often times their struggles were private, and even though this was the life they had chosen, they often had to live with the consequences of their decision alone.

Our objective is to use the real life stories from successful entrepreneurs across different industries and countries as a prescription for how you too can achieve a level of entrepreneurial success realized by only a few in this turbulent economy. Each chapter ended with that leader's rules that guided them through the tough times and served as a beacon when they needed to be heading in the right direction.

Each leader ranks at the highest score for the principles of 24-Hour Leadership. We decided to focus the stories on certain unique aspects of each leader that stood out. For example, we saw these leaders deal with private pain, uncertainty, and triumphs. Every story was about: personal courage, family, small and big victories. The stories include astute strategy and plans, self-confidence, accountability, accurate financial data, sound advice and great intuition that ultimately paid off. These were all strong and outstanding leaders, but one characteristic they all have in common is the willingness to seek and accept help regardless of the source. That help may have come from a business advisor, a friend, or a family member. Equally important was their unwavering commitment to superb communication and the understanding that a big part of everything they have accomplished was as a result of treating people with respect. We saw these leaders create order out of chaos, profits from a mass of red ink, and a high level of individual and team self-confidence out of the ashes of low morale.. That is why their leadership rules were reflective of their dominant styles, preferences, and circumstances.

In this last chapter we have summarized 24-Hour Principles for Business Success that paint an overall picture that combines actions, values, beliefs, and strategies. These principles capture the spirit of these six successful entrepreneurs and point the way for you to immediately start and set the tone for long-term success. We hope you too can achieve your entrepreneurial vision and objectives and build the kind of organization that will endure and make you another great

24-Hour Leader. We provide these principles for success in a question-naire format and scorecard. The purpose of the scorecard is to allow you to self-evaluate your current organization and identify areas of opportunity to build a pathway for improvement. The strategy is to take a hard look at your business as you see it today and assess it against the 24-Hour Principles. An even more robust approach would be to do this as a strategic teambuilding and consensus-building exercise. Ultimately, you will have an analysis that can inform you on where your organization ranks today, what strengths currently exist in the organization, and what areas you should focus on to improve for the future.

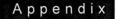

A | 24-Hour Turnaround Scorecard

Part I

Principles for Organizational Success	Principle Score
1. Have a vision and strategic plan that reflects the leader's personality, personal, and family history, ambitions, goals, dreams, industry, and economic reality.	(Assign a score of 0–10 for each of the principles)

1. Have a vision and strategic plan that reflects the leader's personality, personal, and family history, ambitions, goals, dreams, industry, and economic reality.

   – Have a periodic process that independently and thoroughly reviews the market and organizational trends, opportunities, and tasks

   – Continuously review and monitoring of annual goals with quick adjustments to changes

1.

2. Have a clear set of guiding principles and code-of-conduct that all employees know, understand and follow.

   – Demonstrate an unwavering commitment to personal and professional integrity. The leader is the moral compass.

   – Have a consistent leadership style that demonstrates how you want all employees to interact and be treated.

   – Focus on organizational and individual accountability. Have a rewards system consistent with organizational reality. Set objectives and ensure that there are consequences and rewards for doing the right and wrong things.

   – Commit to continuously improving and perfecting the organization with the best personnel who are aligned with current strategy organizational structure.

   – Anticipate and plan for organizational change. Accept the fact that even the best models eventually have to change. Leaders are the catalyst for change

2.

3. Communicate Relentlessly   3.
   - Be visible and accessible to everyone.

   - Constantly clarify, vision, mission, strategy,
     and day-to-day tactics

4. Have a strong financial plan.   4.
   - Dig into the details. Know the numbers and in-
     dicators that can make or break your business.

   - Have a strong strategy to support the funda-
     mentals of your plan.

   - Track the results on daily, weekly, monthly,
     quarterly, and annual basis.

5. Constantly raise the bar. Recognize organi-   5.
   zational and executive development as an
   essential element to success and leadership.

   - Learn from family and life experiences

   - Develop leaders and skills and remember
     everyone is important.

   - Learn from adversity in your life (and from the
     company's history).

   - Learning means improvement and have it part
     of your ongoing efforts to succeed.

6. Be the final decision maker. Don't hesitate to   6.
   get other perspectives when making tough
   decisions.

   - Get the team involved with key decisions,
     where appropriate, and don't hesitate to get
     real support for implementing tough decisions.

   - Leverage your organization as it grows and
     develop other leaders and decision makers

7. Accept help and support. Nobody knows everything.
 	
  – Pick talented, trusted advisors.
 	
  – Put advisors in a position where they can be open and objective.
 	
  – Prepare for personal sacrifice, loneliness, and fear associated with leading an enterprise.
	7.

8. Expect excellence from everyone; in turn provide employees with the tools and professional growth and development opportunities.
 	
  – The best organizations develop from within.
 	
  – Training and development is key to every level of the organization.
 	
  – Mentoring is an accepted part of the culture.
	8.

9. Implement and use technology in the monitoring, management, finance, and growth of your organization.
 	
  – Does your staff embrace using technology to help the company function better.
 	
  – How knowledgeable are your employees at using technology.
 	
  – Do you regularly get outside advice on up to date technologies.
 	
  – The best organizations are utilizing social networking as a means of communicating with all their constituencies.
	9.

10. Facilitate continuous positive action. Plan based on the concept that if the organization is not preparing to grow, then the organization is definitely moving in the wrong direction.
 	
  − The best organizations have strategic planning as a regular process
 	
  − All people are given the opportunity to contribute to the strategic planning process
	10.
	
	TOTAL

Entrepreneurial Score

A total score of:

0–49	The organization is seriously compromised. Take immediate action to address these issues.
50–59	Focus on specific areas of opportunity and take quick action.
60–69	The organization is average and with an action plan can be headed in a more positive direction.
70–79	There are more things going right than wrong. Build on the strengths and find specific areas for improvement.
80–89	A top organization. Use the score to refine the strategic plan and identify how to continue to excel to the top.
90 +	Top functioning organization with an excellent base. Build on success and continue to new heights. Develop strategies to continue benefiting from the current success. Staying on top requires dynamic continuous improvement to stay there.

Part II

For each section list: your score, why you assessed that score, what you regard as strengths in that area, weaknesses and actions.

1. Have a vision and strategic plan that reflects the leader's personality, personal and family history, ambitions, goals, dreams, industry, and economic reality.

   - Have a periodic process that independently and thoroughly reviews the market and organizational trends, opportunities, and tasks.

   - Continuously review and monitoring of annual goals with quick adjustments to changes.

   Score:
   Why:
   Strengths:
   Weaknesses:
   Actions:

2. Have a clear set of guiding principles and code-of-conduct that all employees know, understand and follow.

   - Demonstrate an unwavering commitment to personal and professional integrity. Leader as a moral compass.

   - Have a consistent leadership style that demonstrates how you want all employees to interact and be treated.

   - Focus on organizational and individual accountability. Have a rewards system consistent with organizational reality. Set objectives and ensure that there are consequences and rewards for doing the right and wrong things.

   - Commit to continuously improving and perfecting the organization with the best personnel who are aligned with current strategy organizational structure.

- Anticipate and plan for organizational change. Accept the fact that even the best models eventually have to change. Leaders are the catalyst for change.

Score:
Why:
Strengths:
Weaknesses:
Actions:

3. Communicate Relentlessly.
   - Be visible and accessible to everyone.

   - Constantly clarify, vision, mission, strategy, and day-to-day tactics.

Score:
Why:
Strengths:
Weaknesses:
Actions:

4. Have a strong financial plan.
   - Dig into the details. Know the numbers and indicators that can make or break your business.

   - Have a strong strategy to support the fundamentals of your plan.

   - Track the results on daily, weekly, monthly, quarterly, and annual basis.

Score:
Why:
Strengths:
Weaknesses:
Actions:

5. Constantly raise the bar. Recognize organizational and executive development as an essential element to success and leadership.
   - Learn from family and life experiences.

   - Develop leaders and skills and remember everyone is important.

- Learn from adversity in your life (and from the company's history).
- Leaning means improvement and have it part of your ongoing efforts to succeed.

Score:
Why:
Strengths:
Weaknesses:
Actions:

6. Be the final decision maker. Don't hesitate to get other perspectives when making tough decisions.
   - Get the team involved with key decisions, where appropriate, and don't hesitate to get real support for implementing tough decisions.

   - Leverage your organization as it grows and develop other leaders and decision makers.

Score:
Why:
Strengths:
Weaknesses:
Actions:

7. Accept help and support. Nobody knows everything.
   - Pick talented, trusted advisors.

   - Put advisors in a position where they can be open and objective.

   - Prepare for personal sacrifice, loneliness, and fear associated with leading an enterprise.

Score:
Why:
Strengths:
Weaknesses:
Actions:

8. Expect excellence from everyone; in turn provide employees with the tools and professional growth and development opportunities.

- The best organizations develop from within.
- Training and development is key to every level of the organization.
- Mentoring is an accepted part of the culture.

Score:
Why:
Strengths:
Weaknesses:
Actions:

9. Implement and use technology in the monitoring, management, finance, and growth of your organization.

- Does your staff embrace using technology to help the company function better.

- How knowledgeable are your employees at using technology.

- Do you regularly get outside advice on up to date technologies.

- The best organizations are utilizing social networking as a means of communicating with all their constituencies.

Score:
Why:
Strengths:
Weaknesses:
Actions:

10. Facilitate continuous positive action. Plan based on the concept that if the organization is not preparing to grow, then the organization is definitely moving in the wrong direction.

- The best organizations have strategic planning as a regular process

- All people are given the opportunity to contribute to the strategic planning process

Score:
Why:
Strengths:
Weaknesses:
Actions:

Appendix A: 24-Hour Turnaround Scorecard

About the Authors

Jeffrey S. Davis is CEO and Founder of Mage LLC, one of New England's leading management consulting firms. He's also an adjunct lecturer of entrepreneurship at Olin Graduate School of Business at Babson College and co-hosts the daily business radio show "Mind Your Own Business." A nationally and internationally sought after speaker, Davis is regularly called upon by the business leaders and media as a resource on managing the challenges faced by entrepreneurial and family-run organizations trying to succeed in today's shifting economy. Because of his invaluable experience and track record positioning organizations for rapid growth, change, market leadership and financial success, he sits on the boards of several private and non-profit organizations and has also served as a columnist for the Boston Business Journal. Before founding Mage, Davis established his reputation as an entrepreneurial strategist, organizational change agent, and marketing and sales expert working for well-known international organizations and clients.

JDavis@24-HourTurnaround.com

Mark Cohen, Senior Consultant at Mage LLC, has vast experience as an external consultant and internal human resources leader. His diverse background includes 25 years of working with international and US technology companies in the computer, healthcare, biotechnology and pharmaceutical industries. Cohen's track record includes positions as Worldwide Director of Human Resources at Phillips Medical Systems and a Senior Manager at Maxtor Corporation. He also spent 16 years in human resources management at Digital Equipment Corporation and held training and human resources positions at Fidelity, General Mills and Polaroid.

MCohen@24-HourTurnaround.com

A Message from Happy About®

Thank you for your purchase of this Happy About book. It is available online at http://www.happyabout.com/24hr-turnaround.php or at other online and physical bookstores.

- Please contact us for quantity discounts at sales@happyabout.info
- If you want to be informed by email of upcoming Happy About® books, please email bookupdate@happyabout.info

Happy About is interested in you if you are an author who would like to submit a non-fiction book proposal or a corporation that would like to have a book written for you. Please contact us by email at editorial@happyabout.info or phone (1-408-257-3000).

Other Happy About books available include:

- #CORPORATE CULTURE tweet Book01:
  http://happyabout.com/thinkaha/corporateculturetweet01.php
- #LEADERSHIPtweet Book01:
  http://happyabout.com/thinkaha/projectmanagementtweet01.php
- #COACHING tweet Book01:
  http://www.happyabout.com/thinkaha/coachingtweet01.php
- 42 Rules for Your New Leadership Role:
  http://www.happyabout.com/42rules/yournewleadershiprole.php
- 42 Rules to Increase Sales Effectiveness:
  http://happyabout.com/42rules/increasesaleseffectiveness.php
- 42 Rules for Growing Enterprise Revenue:
  http://happyabout.com/42rules/growing-enterprise-revenue.php
- Managing Sales People:
  http://www.happyabout.com/managingsalespeople.php
- 42 Rules of Employee Engagement:
  http://www.happyabout.com/42rules/employee-engagement.php
- Scrappy General Management:
  http://happyabout.com/scrappyabout/scrappy-general-management.php
- DNA of The Young Entrepreneur:
  http://www.happyabout.com/dna.php
- Competing for Global Dominance:
  http://www.happyabout.com/global-dominance.php
- I'm on LinkedIn (Third Edition)—Now What???:
  http://www.happyabout.com/linkedinhelp.php
- Happy About Extra Hour Every Day:
  http://www.happyabout.com/an-extra-hour.php

A Message from Happy About

Other Happy About® Books

Purchase these books at Happy About http://happyabout.com or at other online and physical bookstores.

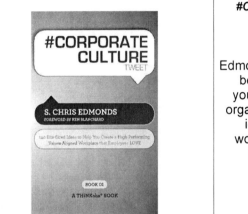

#CORPORATE CULTURE
tweet Book01

In this book, S. Chris Edmonds starts at the very beginning—by showing you how to recognize an organization's culture and identify what a healthy workplace culture looks, acts, and sounds like.

Paperback $19.95
eBook $14.95

42 Rules to Increase Sales Effectiveness

This book upgrades and adjusts foundational rules for today's business environment to increase individual or team overall sales effectiveness.

Paperback $19.95
eBook $14.95

42 Rules for Growing Enterprise Revenue

This book is a brainstorming tool meant to provoke discussion and creativity within executive teams who are looking to boost their top line numbers.

Paperback $19.95
eBook $14.95

Scrappy General Management

This book will provide you with the 7 common sense and repeatable steps that will guide you through running a business that everyone will be proud to be associated with.

Paperback $19.95
eBook $14.95

CPSIA information can be obtained at www.ICGtesting.com
Printed in the USA
269894BV00001B/4/P